The Religious Life of Samuel Johnson

The Religious Life of Samuel Johnson

Charles E. Pierce, Jr.

ARCHON BOOKS

1983

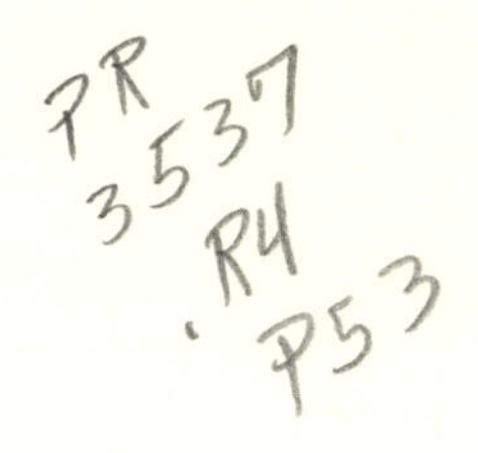

First published 1983 as an Archon Book,
an imprint of The Shoe String Press, Inc.,
Hamden, Connecticut 06514

Printed in the United States of America

Library of Congress Cataloging in Publication Data

Pierce, Charles E.
The religious life of Samuel Johnson.

Bibliography: p.
Includes index.
1. Johnson, Samuel, 1709-1784—Religion and ethics.
2. Authors, English—18th century—Biography.
3. Anglicans—England—Biography. 4. Christian life.
I. Title.
PR3537.R4P53 1983 828'.609 82-13938
ISBN 0-208-01992-8

To
W. Jackson Bate

He, in a sense was spiritually self-conscious, was a tragic figure, i.e. worth putting down as part of the whole of which oneself is part.

Samuel Beckett,
speaking of Samuel Johnson

Shall I, who have been a teacher of others, myself be a castaway?

Samuel Johnson,
speaking to Sir John Hawkins

Contents

Preface 9
Acknowledgments 13
1. *The Anvil of Anxiety* 15
2. *The Crucible of Faith* 34
3. *The Pursuit of Piety* 63
4. *The Character of Fearing* 84
5. *The Meaning of the Journey* 111
6. *A Crisis of Faith* 131
7. *The Last Great Trial* 146
Notes 165
Bibliography 177
Index 179

Preface

No thoughtful reader of Samuel Johnson has ever doubted the truth of Boswell's remark that "the history of his mind as to religion is an important article."[1] Johnson himself made no attempt to conceal the importance of religion for him nor the central place that it occupied in his life. Writing to Queeney Thrale just six months before he died, he exhorted her to "believe a man whose experience has been long, and who can have no wish to deceive you, and who now tells you that the highest honour, and most constant pleasure this life can afford, must be obtained by passing it with attention fixed upon Eternity."[2] Johnson was a deeply religious man who accepted without question the existence of God, who affirmed his faith in the principal truths of Christianity, who was an ardent Church-of-England man, and who sought throughout his life to render himself worthy of salvation. Few commentators have provided a better general sense of Johnson's religion than Boswell in his summary of Johnson's character at the end of the *Life of Samuel Johnson.*

> He was a sincere and zealous Christian, of high Church-of-England and monarchial principles, which he would not tamely suffer to be questioned; and had, perhaps, at an early period, narrowed his mind somewhat too much, both as to religion and politicks. . . . He was steady and inflexible in maintaining the obligations of religion and morality; both from a regard for the order of society, and from a veneration for the Great Source of all order; correct, nay stern in his taste; hard to please, and easily offended; impetuous and irritable in his temper, but of a

> most humane and benevolent heart, which shewed itself not only in a most liberal charity, as far as his circumstances would allow, but in a thousand instances of active benevolence.[3]

And thus it is not surprising that Johnson was celebrated in his own time as much for his piety as for his learning.

> Every line [observed one of his early biographers], every sentiment that issues from his pen, tends to the great centre of all his views, the promotion of virtue, religion, and humanity; nor are his actions less pointed towards the same noble end. Benevolence, charity, and piety are the most striking features in his character, and while his writings point out to us what a good Man *ought to be,* his own conduct sets us an example of what he is.[4]

And in the almost two hundred years since Johnson's death, there has been almost no attempt to qualify or challenge this view of Johnson's religion. The important scholarship on this subject, especially that of the past twenty-five years, has concentrated upon the nature of Johnson's religious thought and has made clear his essential orthodoxy.[5] Maurice Quinlan has convincingly demonstrated that Johnson belonged to the main tradition of English Protestantism that began with Richard Hooker, that was attacked but finally enriched by the turbulent events of the seventeenth century, and that embodied itself in such powerful but diverse figures as Samuel Clarke and William Law in the first quarter of the eighteenth century.[6] And Chester Chapin, following in the steps of Boswell and Quinlan, showed the extent to which Johnson was a true Church-of-England man who accepted with relative ease the central articles of the Anglican faith and who was able to reconcile that faith with the deepest needs of his nature.[7] As a result of this work we have a clear sense of the substance of Johnson's religious belief and of the theological tradition to which he belonged. But we still have no exact knowledge of the place that religion occupied in Johnson's life. We know what he believed but we do not know the effect of that belief upon his life and thought.

The purpose of this study is to give an account of the religious life of Samuel Johnson. It is important to see at the start that Johnson's faith evolved primarily out of a profound psychological need to overcome certain fears about existence that he had acquired as a youth. The combined force of these fears created in him a deep anxiety that he could relieve only by placing his trust in a Christian view of life. But the central irony of Johnson's religious life—and it was a tragic irony—was that Johnson's faith never provided him with the spiritual happiness he sought. It has long been a commonplace to note that Johnson possessed substantial doubts and fears. It has often been suggested, as Bertrand Bronson put it some years ago, that Johnson's "religion was not a mild and sunny element in his life; but crossed with storm and struggle."[8] And yet there has been no thorough analysis of this important struggle, of his doubts about God's ultimate concern for man, of his fears about his own spiritual unworthiness, and of his anguished efforts to lead a better life. It is also important to examine the effect of these religious concerns upon the formation of his complex character, upon the great moral writing that began with *The Vanity of Human Wishes* and ended with *Rasselas,* and upon his moving attempt to make his religion the measure of all the actions of his life. It is perhaps only then that we can realize how important Johnson's faith was to his understanding of himself and how responsible it was for the heroic energy that compelled him to make the most of what he had been given. It is only then that we can be certain that his religious struggle was one of the great pilgrimages of his age.

Acknowledgments

There are, of course, a number of people without whose advice and support I could not have written this book. I wish to thank the members of the Hyder Rollins Committee at Harvard for their aid in the publication of this work. I would like to thank as well the editors of *Eighteenth-Century Studies,* in particular Max Byrd, for permission to reprint material that has already been published. Two of my colleagues, each of whom read a draft of this book, deserve special thanks. Julia McGrew has been a steadfast and kind friend who encouraged me to go on when it often seemed easier to give up. And Dean T. Mace has enriched more than one afternoon of my life by his wit, urbanity, and intelligence. I would also like to thank Jacques Barzun, who long ago set out to help me "weed the garden of my prose" and who ever since has always somehow found time "to read me." No one knows better than my wife, Barbara, how much I have depended upon her. Without the support of this "dearest of dear ladies," I might well have faltered.

My deepest debt, however, is to W. Jackson Bate, who introduced me years ago to Johnson and to the serious study of literature. It was he who first showed me the connection between art and life. It was he who first encouraged me to acquire a moral education. It is he who still haunts my mind as he quotes Whitehead to the effect that all moral education is "impossible apart from the habitual vision of greatness." Little does he realize how much he has become for many of us in this generation the image of such greatness and the instrument of such an education. I dedicate this book to him.

1

The Anvil of Anxiety

1
The Anvil of Anxiety

The man with the clear head is the man who . . . looks life in the face, realizes that everything in it is problematic, and feels himself lost. And this is the simple truth—that to live is to feel oneself lost—he who accepts it has already begun to find himself, to be on firm ground. Instinctively, as do the shipwrecked, he will look round for something to which to cling, and that tragic, ruthless glance, absolutely sincere, because it is a question of his salvation, will cause him to bring order into the chaos of his life. These are the only genuine ideas; the ideas of the shipwrecked. All the rest is rhetoric, posturing, farce. He who does not really feel himself lost, is without remission; that is to say, he never finds himself, never comes up against his own reality.

Ortega y Gasset, *The Revolt of the Masses*

Samuel Johnson was not an instinctively religious man. He was by nature a rationalist who was always happiest when he was employing his reason to cut through cant and to arrive at truth. He was also by nature a skeptic, always doubting what others held to be true until such propositions were validated in the court of reason or experience. Johnson, however, became a profoundly religious person out of psychological need, out of the need to overcome his sense of the misery of life and out of his desire to give his own life meaning and direction. Convinced that life was at best very uncertain and at worst very unhappy, and determined not to surrender to despair, Johnson turned to the Christian view of life, and in particular to the Anglican expression of that view, as the principal means by which he could most satisfactorily endure "the pain of being a man." As he put the matter to Boswell in 1778, "without asserting Stoicism, it may be said, that it is our business to exempt ourselves as much as we can from the power of external things. There is but one solid basis of happiness; and that is, the reasonable hope of a happy futurity."[1] And his belief, as all who knew him affirmed, became one of the central elements of his character, responsible in many large and important ways for much of what he thought and did. As Boswell himself remarked in his fine protrait of Johnson at the end of the *Life*, "his piety [was] constant, and the ruling principle of all his conduct."[2] It influenced what he read, how he spent his time, what he believed to be the purpose of art, and ultimately how he understood life itself. It led him to believe that "the business of life was to work out our salvation."[3] Although his belief helped to allay doubts and to provide much needed solace, nevertheless it also afflicted him with additional fears, some of which were theological and some of which were spiritual. The former related to Johnson's struggle to understand the nature and workings of divine providence while the latter pertained to his lifelong fear that he might never prove worthy of redemption. These fears proved to be so persistent and so profound that Johnson spent far more of his life in a state of fear and trembling than has been generally recognized. Much of his enormous energy was vitiated by his agonizing battle against melancholy and depression, against madness and despair. In order to understand fully, then, the complex nature of his belief as well as its effect upon his life and art it is necessary to examine with great care the process by which he struggled to ease his fears through acceptance of a Christian view of life.

2

Johnson's deepest fear about existence was that it had no clear meaning, that there was no certain basis upon which to enjoy life. The result was, as Imlac had remarked in *Rasselas*, that "human life is every where a state in which much is to be endured and little to be enjoyed."[4] Although Johnson himself made no attempt to conceal his dark view of existence, nevertheless many of his contemporaries found it disturbing and tried to play down its influence or dismiss it altogether.[5] More recently, serious readers of Johnson have acknowledged his essential pessimism but have sought to mitigate it by stressing his "zest for life," his humor and courage, and his sharp sense of the difference between real and imaginary evils.[6] But it is important to recognize at the outset the depth of this conviction and to realize, as I shall try to demonstrate more fully later on, the extent to which his vitality, his laughter, his common sense, and his courage all evolved in response to what he once described as "the sorrow inherent in humanity." They were all attempts to divert himself from further reflection upon man's painful condition; they were all defenses erected against the fear that life was at heart an anguished journey into the unknown.

The ultimate origin of this dark view of human life derived from Johnson's own experience, from those formative early years that began in Lichfield and ended with his unhappy departure from Oxford. For it was during this period that Johnson started to acquire his sense of how complex, problematic, and uncertain life was. He felt for the first time how difficult it was to comprehend life's meaning and to order his own accordingly. The romances he devoured as a child suggested he had embarked on some sort of journey or quest, but he understood neither the nature of the quest nor the end of the journey. And he had received so little useful help in charting his course that by the time he left Oxford he was, to take up Ortega's metaphor, "shipwrecked." He was lost on life's sea, adrift and alone, helpless and disconsolate. He had looked life in the face and had been overwhelmed with anxiety by what he had seen. But before we can analyze his response to this anxiety we must take a fresh look at the circumstances that brought him to this psychological impasse.

3

Johnson could well have used Pope's phrase "this long disease my life" to describe his own. From his near-fatal birth to his death seventy-five years later, he scarcely passed a day in which he did not suffer from some physical discomfort or disease. Most of these ailments first appeared when he was a very young child, before he was three, and continued to afflict him in erratic intervals and in one form or another for the rest of his life. Speaking of the circumstances of his birth, Johnson wrote in his diary, "I was born almost dead, and could not cry for some time," and then after relating the reactions of his parents to his arrival and describing his early infirmities, he concluded, "in ten weeks I was taken home, a poor, diseased infant, almost blind." Shortly thereafter, he was afflicted with scrofula, a tubercular infection of the glands of the neck, which necessitated an operation which left scars that permanently disfigured his face. And if this had not been enough for a very young boy to endure, Johnson then caught smallpox, which further marred his appearance. Thus by the time he was three or four, he was deaf in one ear, blind in one eye, with his face disfigured by scrofula and pitted by smallpox. It is no wonder that Dr. Swinfen, his godfather, "used to say, that he never knew any child reared with so much difficulty."[7] Although James Clifford was right to point out that "Johnson appears to have taken a fierce delight in stressing his own early troubles," and although the young Johnson rapidly grew into a robust and even strong man, he never enjoyed consistent good health or a pleasing appearance.[8] And these facts had serious and lasting consequences upon his outlook. His flawed personal appearance destined him from an early age to be an outsider and to feel uncomfortable in many social situations. This discomfort increased as he grew up and as his nervous tics, shabby attire, and uncouth manners made him an object of ridicule. And his ongoing struggle against ill health deepened his fundamental uncertainty about life, intensified his fear of death, and increased his preoccupation with time. It made him realize how short life was, how death could cut him down at any point, and how he must make the most of the time allotted to him. He began to feel for the first time the essential transiency, if not vanity, of human life, of how "we act as if life were without end, though we see and confess its uncertainty and shortness." And he became convinced, as he would later put it, that he who "has already trifled away those months and years, in which he should have laboured, must remember that he has now only a part of that of which the whole is little; and that since the few moments remaining are to be considered as the last trust of heaven, not one is to be lost."[9]

4

Of equal importance in the development of his anxiety were his relations with his parents and the effect of their unhappy marriage upon him. We now know a good deal more than Boswell and the early commentators about Johnson's ambivalence toward his parents. James Clifford, drawing largely upon Boswell, has made clear how the young Johnson was "intellectually drawn to [his father] but emotionally repelled," how he was attracted to his father's general learning, knowledge of Latin, and love of books but often embarrassed by his father's attempt to show him off, resentful of the melancholy he believed he had inherited from his father, and depressed by his father's failure to manage his professional affairs properly.[10] George Irwin has also made a provocative case for the deeply ambivalent feelings Johnson developed toward his mother: how he loved her for the comfort and instruction that she gave him but came to hate her for the fears and guilt she unconsciously inspired.[11] Although he may have inherited his love of learning from his father and his piety from his mother, nevertheless he also acquired from them, at least so he believed, his chronic sense of the misery of life as well as his obsession always to do his best. (It could well be said of Johnson what he later said of Pope, namely, that his ruling passion was "his desire for excellence.") He acquired from them the two demons, melancholy and guilt, which were to curse him throughout his life. And it was the power of these two forces, more than any others, that prevented Johnson in later life from ever enjoying prolonged periods of happiness.

Johnson was also deeply affected by the unhappy marriage of his parents. He grew up in a family of emotional strife, economic instability, and social rivalry. In a private journal that he began in 1734 to record the notable persons and events of his early life, Johnson set down the only lengthy comment he ever made about his parents' marriage:

> My father and mother had not much happiness from each other. They seldom conversed; for my father could not bear to talk of his affairs; and my mother, being unacquainted with books, cared not to talk of any thing else. Had my mother been more literate, they had been better companions. She might have sometimes introduced her unwelcome topick with more success, if she could have diversified her conversation. Of business she had no distinct conception; and therefore her discourse was composed only of complaint, fear, and suspicion. Neither of them ever tried to calculate the profits of

> trade, or the expenses of living. My mother concluded that we were poor, because we lost by some of our trades; but the truth was, that my father, having in the early part of his life contracted debts, never had trade sufficient to enable him to pay them, and maintain his family; he got something, but not enough. It was not til about 1768, that I thought to calculate the returns of my father's trade, and by that estimate his probable profits. This, I believe, my parents never did.[12]

Implicit in this commentary is Johnson's belief that much of his parents' unhappiness could have been eliminated if his father had been able to overcome his guilt at being a poor provider and if his mother had been able to conduct herself in a more helpful and responsible way. But neither of his parents proved able to do this. And the result was a marriage of little love and much bickering, a home that resembled "the house of discord" that Johnson described Pertinax inhabiting in *Rambler* 95.[13]

The effect of these tensions upon Johnson was complex and profound. He had witnessed firsthand the difficulties of human communication and the strains of marriage; and he had come to understand how much of the unhappiness of human life arose directly from man's inability to manage his simple domestic affairs.[14] It was vital, as he later made clear in his portrait of Gelidus, for the scholar and indeed for every man to attend to the duties of common life; for "the first attention is due to practical virtue."[15] And it was no accident that years later he took up this theme again and again in his great moral writing.[16] Johnson also realized how much of human misery was thus self-created, how much it derived from man's failure to free himself from the prison of his self-serving desires. He saw how difficult it was to know oneself, how hard to recognize one's weaknesses and vices, how painful but necessary to overcome them. And all of this forced him to admit that happiness was elusive and that misery was the natural state of man.

5

If observation of his parents' strained marriage had made the young Johnson realize how much of human misery was self-created, then his abbreviated stay at Oxford forced him to acknowledge how much he was at the mercy of forces beyond his control. When he first came up to Oxford at nineteen, he was a gifted but callow youth from the Midlands who like many undergraduates, then and now, had no clear sense of himself, of his possible occupation, of the values by which he could conduct his life. Having distinguished himself as a brilliant student at the schools in Lichfield and having held his own with his witty and worldly uncle, Cornelius Ford, Johnson set out for Oxford, as John Wain has wonderfully described, with high hopes and great expectations.[17] He longed to escape at least for a while the tensions of his family and the constraints of provincial life. But from almost the moment he arrived he was frustrated and unhappy. Years later, when he talked of this period of his life, he made no attempt to conceal his unhappiness and even went out of his way to dispel any sentimental image of himself as a carefree student who, when he was not attending lectures, was irreverently stirring up his peers to acts of rebellion. As he told Boswell, "Ah, Sir, I was mad and violent. It was bitterness which they mistook for frolick. I was miserably poor, and I thought to fight my way by my literature and my wit; so I disregarded all power and all authority."[18]

This bitterness derived almost entirely from Johnson's growing awareness of how disadvantaged he was in comparison with many of those around him. While he was poor, provincial, and powerless, many of his contemporaries were wealthy, worldly, and well connected. He had nothing but his learning and wit by which to secure a place in the world while many of his peers, possessed of substantially inferior talents, still seemed to have promising opportunities. Oxford thus produced much frustration in Johnson as he came to feel how difficult it was to escape from his impoverished and narrowing background and to make his way in the world by the sheer power of his mind. It was thus not just false pride that caused him to reject a pair of new shoes that had been left at his door by some thoughtful friend.[19] To accept them would have been to admit not only that he was "miserably poor" but that he could not help himself. What he increasingly resented at Oxford was the notion that he could not shape his own life; so he resisted most attempts by the university to determine how he should conduct himself. His failure to attend some of his tutor's lectures was a symbolic protest against the imposition of authority, against his right to determine his needs and interests. What Johnson sought was economic and intellectual independence; what he found was just the reverse. He was a prisoner of his own circumstances. And there was no more painful manifestation of that truth than when his family proved unable to pay for his education and thus cut short his residence at Oxford after only thirteen months.

Johnson himself never expressed what he felt upon his premature departure from Oxford; his only comment upon it was to record in Latin in his diary that he had left in December 1729.[20] But it is not hard to imagine the disappointment he must have felt in leaving, in surrendering, at least for the moment, his dream of a more independent and cultured existence. Although his time at Oxford had not been uniformly pleasant, its possibilities were far more appealing than those to which he knew he was returning in Lichfield. To return home, after so short a time, inevitably meant a rapid reinvolvement in the discordant life of his parents and in the precarious state of his father's business. This prospect was painful enough. What was even more distressing was an inevitable self-confrontation in which Johnson had to face, if not resolve, some crucial questions. What could he now do? How could he support himself? These were his immediate concerns; but there were others that continued to haunt him just as much, even if they seemed on the surface less pressing. How could he make use of the talents he possessed now that a university education had been denied him? How could he escape from the poverty that had dogged him and distinguish himself in the world beyond Lichfield? How, in short, could he give meaning and direction to his life?

6

The urgency of these questions and his inability to answer them plunged Johnson, either shortly before he left Oxford or shortly thereafter, into an acute depression, or what Boswell later described as a "horrible hypochondria, with perpetual irritation, fretfulness, and impatience; and with a dejection, gloom, and despair, which made existence misery. He suffered extraordinary lassitude, was unable "to distinguish the hour upon the town-clock," and feared for the first time the onset of insanity.[21] We do not know the exact cause of this first serious depression since

Johnson again said very little about it. Boswell attributed it to "the morbid melancholy" that Johnson felt he had inherited from his father, while Katharine Balderston has more sensibly suggested that Johnson's encounter with the rigorous spiritual demands of William Law's *Serious Call to a Devout and Holy Life* "was at least a contributing cause of the serious attack of depression which began in December 1729."[22]

The main cause of this breakdown, however, was neither his chronic melancholy nor his reading of Law, though both were important catalysts, but rather his anxiety about the nature of life itself or what he called "the radical misery of life." And the key word of this important phrase was *radical*, which Johnson used in its strict Latinate sense to mean "original" or "implanted by nature." Life could be seen and felt but it defied analysis; it resisted all attempts to be managed in some substantial and comprehensible way. Neither his parents nor his teachers, neither his mentors nor his peers, had been able to provide him with any workable solution to the riddle. And his own efforts had been frustrated at every turn by his impoverished circumstances. The attempt to give his existence significance, like the pursuit of pleasure, seemed doomed to end in frustration. His own experience at Oxford had illustrated that truth. Johnson had been forced to conclude that the misery of life was ineradicable.

His own efforts to escape from this terrifying Slough of Despond were a characteristic mixture of physical purgation and psychiatric therapy—the long walks to Birmingham and the searching self-analysis submitted to Dr. Swinfen.[23] But these were all in vain. They may have afforded him momentary relief, but nearly a year after he left Oxford he was still suffering from depression. At this time, that is in late 1730 or early 1731, Johnson managed to rouse himself from his despondency through the aid of religion. Talking with Boswell and Anna Seward on April 29, 1783, of the large number of people who live without religion Johnson remarked: "Sir, you need not wonder at this, when you consider how large a proportion of almost every man's life is passed without thinking of it. I myself was for some years totally regardless of religion. It had dropped out of my mind. It was at an early part of my life. Sickness brought it back, and I hope I have never lost it since."[24] And thus Chester Chapin is right to argue that "sickness is probably to be given equal weight with the eloquence of Law as a factor in Johnson's rediscovery of religion."[25] In order to understand, however, the full significance of Johnson's return to religion in this way at this time, it is critical that we review what we know of his religious life up to this moment.

7

Boswell has described three stages in the early development of Johnson's religious life.[26] The central figure of the first stage was certainly his mother, who took her own faith seriously and who was determined that her firstborn son should do likewise. It was she who, when Johnson was just three years old, "first informed [him] of a future state." Recalling the scene with great vividness nearly thirty years later, he wrote: "I remember, that being in bed with my mother one morning, I was told by her of the two places to which the inhabitants of this world were received after death; one a fine place filled with happiness, called Heaven; the other a *sad* place, called Hell."[27] Much critical attention has been devoted to this passage as the earliest, if not the ultimate, source of Johnson's well-known fear of death and damnation. James Clifford has best summarized this point of view: "If he was too young at this time to grasp the full significance of what his mother was saying, she must subsequently have made the dangers of future punishment clear enough. Sarah's approach to the Bible was literal and devout. . . . Hell was real, and damnation no mere symbolic device. So well did her son learn the lesson that he was never rid of the terrors of the other world."[28]

But Johnson himself drew no such conclusion. He simply remarked in his own account of this experience, "that this account much affected my imagination, I do not remember. When I was risen, my mother bade me repeat what she had told me to Thomas Jackson. When I told this afterwards to my mother, she seemed to wonder that she should begin such talk so late as that the first time could be remembered."[29] We should not thus read too much into this experience since Johnson himself did not stress the significance and since it represents an exchange that was undoubtedly repeated in many Christian families with no more profound effect than it had had upon Johnson.

We should not miss, however, the seriousness with which Sarah Johnson approached this issue nor the important place she felt religion should occupy in the development of her son's character. She had clearly felt it imperative to introduce her son as early as possible, long before he was capable of clear understanding and rational inquiry, to the great mysteries of Christianity. She may well have told him stories of this kind in her effort to impress upon him the value of the Christian life. (We may recall the familiar account of her instructing Johnson to learn his prayers by heart at an early age and his extraordinary mastery of them on the spot.) We know, furthermore, that once Johnson had learned how to read, his mother forced him to read each Sunday a chapter from *The Whole Duty of Man*. Though he found the obligatory perusal of this well-known religious handbook unconvincing and worthless, nevertheless the fact that he read it at all is a testimony to his mother's influence.

On the basis of these few anecdotes it would be easy to depict Sarah Johnson as an inflexible and stern woman who took her religion soberly and who was determined to impress it upon her son. The truth is that she was not so much a latter-day Calvinist as she was an earnest, devout, unimaginative Anglican, who had been a lifelong believer and who wished to make sure that her son became one as well. But we can see in retrospect that the greatest influence that she exerted upon the religious education of her son derived not from any single lesson she taught him but rather from her conviction of the central place that the Christian faith should occupy in human life.

8

We do not know as much as we should like about the second major stage of Johnson's religious development, as defined by Boswell, that is, from when he was about nine to when he went up to Oxford at nineteen. What we do know suggests that it was a period of general indifference to religion and that it fell into two distinct phases. In the first, as he told Boswell, "I fell into an inattention to religion, or an indifference about it, in my ninth year. The church at Lichfield, in which we had a seat, wanted reparation, so I was to go and find a seat in other churches; and having bad eyes, and being awkward about this, I used to go and read in the fields on Sunday. This habit continued till my fourteenth year; and still I find a great reluctance to go to church."[30]

This statement, as it stands in the *Life*, can easily be misinterpreted to mean that Johnson became indifferent to religion itself; rather, it means that he ceased to attend church regularly on Sundays. Johnson's explanation was in fact valid since Saint Mary's was undergoing some badly needed repairs at the time and since Johnson himself could neither see nor hear the service as well as he liked. (These latter infirmities continued to discourage Johnson from regular attendance at church in later life.) What is noteworthy about this passage is that the dominant psychological pattern of his religious life had already been established. His profound sense of religious duty, largely derived from his mother but now increasingly internalized, had already proved weaker than he had hoped and had produced guilt, which he sought to relieve by reading, most probably passages from the Bible or from the *Book of Common Prayer*.

It was also about this time that Johnson started to think more critically about Christianity than he ever had before and experienced his first serious doubts about its truths. Mrs. Thrale records that

> at the age of ten years his mind was disturbed by scruples of infidelity, which preyed upon his spirits, and made him very uneasy; the more so, as he revealed his uneasiness to no one, being naturally (as he said) "of a sullen temper and reserved disposition." He searched, however, diligently but fruitlessly, for evidences of the truth of revelation; and at length recollecting a book he had once seen in his father's shop, intitled, *De Veritate Religionis, etc.* he began to think himself highly culpable for neglecting such a means of information, and took himself severely to task for this sin, adding many acts of voluntary, and to others unknown, penance. The first opportunity which offered (of course) he seized the book with avidity; but on examination, not finding himself scholar enough to peruse its contents, set his heart at rest; and, not thinking to enquire whether there were any English books written on the subject, followed his usual amusements, and considered his conscience as lightened of a crime. He redoubled his diligence to learn the language that contained the information he most wished for; but from the pain which guilt had given him,

he now began to deduce the soul's immortality, which was the point that belief first stopped at; and from that moment resolving to be a Christian, became one of the most zealous and pious ones our nation ever produced."[31]

What we see here is not only Johnson's fierce pride but his stubborn determination to find rational proof or incontrovertible evidence for the truth of revelation. Too ashamed to admit his "infidelity" and too proud to seek insight from a friend, he did what he so often did in later life. He pored through many books until he found one that spoke to the question that haunted him. This anecdote is thus the first instance of what became his ruling passion in all discussions of the most important questions of religion, namely, the need to have as much evidence as possible on the given issue. Everything, but especially the truths of Christianity, must be examined carefully and must be tested by reason and experience. It is no wonder that years later he testily dismissed Hume's claim to novelty in certain religious questions by remarking that "every thing which Hume has advanced against Christianity had passed through my mind long before he wrote."[32] We do not know precisely when Johnson did the critical thinking that allowed him to push Hume aside with such disdain, but it may well have been undertaken in his early teens.

9

This initial phase soon gave way, however, to a very different period in which, as Johnson remarked to Boswell: "I then became a sort of lax *talker* against religion, for I did not much *think* against it; and this lasted till I went to Oxford, where it would not be *suffered.*"[33] The full significance of this remark can be grasped only when we recall Johnson's age and when we understand his distinction, articulated here for the first time but practiced throughout his life, between talking and thinking. Johnson had just entered adolescence and was in the process of discovering and enjoying his unusual intellectual powers. He had already distinguished himself as an excellent student at the Lichfield Grammar School, where he had acquired a sound knowledge of Latin and "of all ancient writers." Unable to make a place for himself by his athletic prowess or his personal charm, he made his way by his intelligence and conversation. He might well remind us, as he talked loftily to his schoolmates after a class of instruction in the catechism, of Stephen Dedalus's high-handed discourse to his helpless peers on Aquinas's theory of beauty. Johnson, like Dedalus, desired more to be admired than to state the truth, more to be impressive than informative. He had begun to talk for victory.

It is thus important not to read too much into this confession of religious indifference, in part because it was brief and in part because it was not profound. The key words of the utterance are "lax talker," which suggest that Johnson saw himself not as heretical but rhetorical. He was not flirting with atheism but rather revelling in the power of his own mind to play with words and ideas in an irreverent and witty way. And it should also be remembered that when he was seventeen he wrote one of his most overtly religious works, "Upon the Feast of St. Simon and St. Jude," which, for a poet who came to have serious doubts about the composition of religious poetry, reveals an intense faith in the power of Christ to raise "the barb'rous nations" from their fall. As James Clifford has remarked, "though [Johnson] might still on occasion speak slightingly of the church and was 'lax' in his thinking, there was within him a passionate depth of submerged religious feeling."[34] This feeling, which Johnson had acquired from his mother, first fully came to the surface at Oxford.

10

The thirteen months that Johnson spent at Oxford marked the third stage of his early religious development and "went a great way towards fixing," as Sir John Hawkins observed, "as well his moral as his literary character." For it was then that Johnson understood the central place that his faith could—and should—occupy in his life. As Hawkins went on to point out, "the order and discipline of a college life, the reading the best authors, the attendance on public exercises, the early calls to prayer, the frequent instructions from the pulpit, with all the other means of religious and moral improvement, had their proper effect; and though they left his natural temper much as they found it, they begat in his mind those sentiments of piety which were the rule of his conduct throughout his future life, and made so conspicuous a part of his character."[35] But such measures would have had little effect upon his future religious life if he had not also encountered William Law's moving exhortation to the religious life. Johnson picked up *A Serious Call to a Devout and Holy Life* "expecting to find it a dull book, (as such books generally are,) and perhaps to laugh at it. But I found Law quite an overmatch for me; and this was the first occasion of my thinking in earnest of religion, after I became capable of rational inquiry."[36] Law's book is a minor masterpiece but it could not have had such a profound effect upon Johnson unless it had spoken directly to his psychological needs. Its appeal to Johnson lay in the fact that it addressed the central problem of his life: how to understand and manage the anguished condition in which he found himself.

Law addressed all men and women who were already practicing Christians but who wished to draw nearer to that standard of Christian perfection exemplified in the life of Christ. He was not trying to convert a nonbeliever into a believer, but a believer into a more devout disciple or, as some have suggested, into a saint. His mission was not one of conversion but of purification. He sought to persuade the convinced Christian to pursue the Christian life with greater devotion and with greater discipline. Johnson was thus a perfect candidate for Law's spiritual regimen. Having undergone a period of relative indifference, Johnson was just the kind of lapsed Christian whom Law sought to reach.

Law's subject, furthermore, as set forth in his title, must have appealed to Johnson because he exhorted the complacent believer to make his faith the center of his life. The key word in the title is "life," and by it Law meant man's everyday existence with all of its boredom, confusion, and uncertainty. His main concern was to convince the reader of "the necessity of a devout spirit, or habit of mind, in every part of our common life, in the discharge of all our business, in the use of all the gifts of God."[37] His aim was not to divorce religion from man's worldly pursuits but rather to see these pursuits in a Christian context. Thus after a careful catalogue of all the "virtues and holy tempers of Christianity," Law concludes that "they are not ours unless they be the virtues and tempers of our ordinary life."[38]

Johnson would have responded sympathetically to this argument since it showed him the way to integrate his religious values with his secular needs. And he found this conviction even more compelling because of Law's insistence on grounding man's

Christian faith in the soil of psychological experience. To Johnson, Law was an eloquent moral realist who had a profound sense of man's capacity for self-deception and sin. In his gentle satiric portraits of various human vices, Law revealed a shrewd knowledge of the temptations men and women experience as well as a keen comprehension of the way in which we rationalize our pursuit of what is pleasing and profitable to us. He argued that the failure of most men to lead a life dedicated to Christian virtue was due less to man's innate sinfulness than to the triumph of human passion. At the end of his exposition of human pride and vanity, Law wrote: "I have just touched upon these absurd characters, for no other end but to convince you, in the plainest manner, that the strictest rules of religion are so far from rendering a life dull, anxious, and uncomfortable . . . that, on the contrary, all the miseries, vexations, and complaints, that are in the world, are owing to want of religion; being directly caused by those absurd passions which religion teaches us to deny."[39]

These remarks must have seemed to Johnson as if they were directed at his own inability to reconcile his religious needs with his passional nature. They offered a persuasive explanation of the hold that some passions had upon him. But they also offered a kind of solace; for implicit in all that Law wrote was his conviction that man could triumph over these forces and could redirect his life by the vigorous performance of acts of Christian devotion. And it may well have been Law's conviction that religious discipline helped not only to moderate our passions but also to create our greatest human happiness that was the ultimate appeal of this work for Johnson. "So true it is," Law asserted, "that the more we live by the rules of religion, the more peaceful and happy do we render our lives."[40] It is thus no wonder that Johnson found himself overwhelmed by this work; for it had met him on his own terms and showed him how he could give meaning to his life.

It is easy to imagine the appeal that this little book must have had for Johnson, but it is more difficult to assess its precise effect upon him. Boswell was the first to argue that *A Serious Call* acted as a spiritual stimulus when he observed that "from this time forward, religion was the predominant object of his thoughts." And he was also the first critic of Johnson's religion to note that this work, which Johnson later described as "the finest piece of hortatory theology in any language," also caused him much unhappiness, "though, with the just sentiments of a conscientious christian, he [Johnson] lamented that his practice of its duties fell far short of what it ought to be."[41] Maurice Quinlan concluded his discussion of Law's influence upon Johnson by essentially agreeing with Boswell's original estimate and by arguing that *A Serious Call* had "helped to develop his deep sense of religion" as well as "to contribute to his fears that he might not be saved."[42]

I would concur with both of these judgments but I would stress what Johnson himself said about its influence, namely, that it was responsible for the first serious thinking he had done about religion since his early teens. Law's vision of human nature and of human life set Johnson to thinking in earnest of his own faith and of the place that it could occupy in his existence. But *A Serious Call* was not solely responsible for Johnson's decision to make his faith the center of his life from this time forward. Law's treatise had prepared the way, but it was, as Chester Chapin has rightly argued, the vicissitudes of Johnson's own life that completed what Law had begun.[43] It was the harrowing experience of his own breakdown that made Johnson realize his profound need for religion.

11

Sickness brought religion back into Johnson's life because it made him realize that he possessed neither the physical nor the psychological strength to contend with the overwhelming demands of life. It created in him the horrific fear that life might be incomprehensible and meaningless. Johnson did not cry out, as Kurtz did at the end of his life in *Heart of Darkness*, "the horror! the horror!" but he may well have thought "the terror, the terror" as he sat in the town square staring, unseeing, at the town clock. Johnson obviously felt a fear of life as profound and powerful as his fear of death. He had arrived at Ortega's "simple truth" that "to live is to feel oneself lost." And in accepting this truth as an inescapable fact, Johnson prepared the way for his rescue. Instinctively, to use Ortega's words, Johnson looked around "for something to which to cling, and that tragic, ruthless glance, absolutely sincere, because it [was] a question of salvation, [caused] him to bring order into the chaos of his life."[44] Johnson realized that he had two choices. He could surrender to despair or he could seek to discover some means by which to endure the terror of life and at the same time give his existence meaning.

Johnson's solution was to turn, or perhaps more accurately, to return to the Anglican faith, to the faith of his mother, of his childhood, of *A Serious Call*. He turned to it because it best answered his psychological needs. It offered the best explanation of the misery of life and the most satisfactory account of its possible meaning. It offered him solace and a *raison d'être*, and it held out, above all, the hope that he could conduct his life in a way that could bring him real happiness and peace of mind.

Johnson did not realize at the time of this first great depression the causal relationship between his psychological fears and his turning to religion. He could not see then the extent to which his admission of his own weakness had forced him to face life as it is, as well as to seek a genuine solution to what baffled and pained him. His harrowing experience had in fact exposed him to new possibilities, to new ways of coming to terms with life. By admitting his weakness, he acknowledged his need to be helped by a superior force. By admitting his confusion, he acknowledged his need for a comprehensive and sustaining view of life. It was not until years later, not until the final decade of his life, that Johnson indicated that he understood the extent to which his intense faith had arisen in reaction to his fear of life, to his dread of despair. In one of the late entries of his diary, Johnson jotted down in the middle of a list of otherwise mundane things, "Faith in some proportion to Fear."[45] It is not clear from its immediate context what this statement means, but it expresses for me Johnson's conscious recognition that his faith had largely developed in response to his oldest and deepest fear that life was meaningless. This suggestive remark is the clearest admission that Johnson ever made that his faith—and indeed all that was central to his character and conduct—was from start to finish forged on the anvil of existential anxiety.

What Johnson thus dimly perceived at the end of his life was what later became the principal point in Kierkegaard's greatest writing, namely, as Ernest Becker has nicely summarized it, the extent to which "one goes through it all to arrive at faith, the faith that one's very creatureliness has some meaning to a Creator; that despite one's true insignificance, weakness, death, one's existence has meaning in some ultimate sense because it exists within an eternal and infinite scheme of things brought about and maintained to some kind of design by some creative force."[46] Johnson recognized in retrospect that while his fears had paralyzed him and had brought him to despair they also had opened him up to a radically new way of conceiving life, to a radically new understanding of the place of faith in human life. He recognized, as Kierkegaard made clear in *The Sickness unto Death,* that to experience despair fully is not a disadvantage but rather the ultimate opportunity for self-realization. For only after experiencing such anxiety can one realize the need to struggle for what Kierkegaard called "a theological self," that self which stands "directly in the sight of God." It was this self that Johnson set out to acquire and that he revealed most poignantly in his prayers and meditations.

The ultimate effect of Johnson's sickness, then, was not only to bring the religion of his youth back to him but to make his faith the center of his life. It produced what amounted to a conversion, not of the sort that he had defined in the *Dictionary* as "a change from reprobation to grace, from a bad to a holy life," but more like the state that William James described in which a man's "religious ideas, previously peripheral in his consciousness, now take a central place, and . . . form the habitual centre of his energy."[47] The Christian ideas that Johnson had acquired early in his youth but that to a large extent had remained suppressed throughout his adolescence now emerged in full and intense form to unify his character and to direct his life.

Throughout his early life, but particularly at Oxford, Johnson had been engaged in a quest for a rational explanation of the nature of things. In this pursuit he had devoured Greek literature, read metaphysics, dabbled in philosophy, and steeped himself in the Church Fathers. None of them had fulfilled his need; none of them had been able to provide him with a satisfactory account of life. It was not until he read *A Serious Call* and not until he experienced his terrifying breakdown that Johnson realized how much he needed his faith to give his life significance. By 1731 the Christian view of life, and especially Law's astringent version [illegible]med a central place in Johnson's character and had [illegible]ard parts of his troubled soul. By commit[illegible]al of Christian perfection, he was able to [illegible] this earth as preparation for an afterlife in [illegible] view all that he said and did as an essential [illegible] to regain divine grace and obtain salvation.

2

The Crucible of Faith

The knowledge of God without that of man's misery causes pride. The knowledge of man's misery without that of God causes despair.

Pascal, *Pensées*

The tragic irony of Johnson's religious life was that the faith to which he turned to rescue himself from despair rapidly created within him its own anxieties. His faith helped to relieve his existential *angst* but it also produced certain doubts and fears that deeply troubled him. We must realize that the man at the Club who argued passionately for Christianity as "the highest perfection of humanity" often became at home a lonely figure wracked by doubt and haunted by fears of his own unworthiness.[1] It is thus no longer possible to view Johnson's faith as a triumph of rationalistic piety nor to accept the claim that "at all major points Johnson finds Christian doctrine and teaching so exactly consonant to the human condition that it is difficult to assume impulses in him constantly at war with his faith."[2] That Johnson's faith was orthodox cannot be denied; that this orthodoxy was in complete accord with his own nature and that it provoked no internal resistance must be largely doubted. For a close examination of Johnson's religious thinking makes clear that he possessed doubts, that these doubts created fears, and that these fears afflicted him throughout his life. It is also clear that Johnson had a much more difficult time trying to sustain his faith than has bee[illegible] generally acknowledged. Only after we have grasped the tensi[illegible] inherent in his religious thought and have witnessed the st[illegible] he endured to sustain his faith can we realize the degree [illegible] his character—and indeed all that he undertook—was [illegible] crucible of faith.

2

Johnson never had much difficulty in accepting the existence of God. Naturally distrustful of metaphysical speculation and deeply convinced of the limitations of human reason, Johnson accepted with complete confidence the traditional argument for a First Cause.[3] He also had little trouble in proving to his satisfaction that the God of Nature was the God of Revelation. In this endeavor he was substantially aided by reading Hugo Grotius, Samuel Clarke, and John Pearson, all of whom he later recommended to any man "whose faith is yet unsettled."[4] Grotius in *De Veritate Religionis Christi*, Pearson in *An Exposition of the Creed*, and Clarke in *A Demonstration of the Being and Attributes of God* all express, as S. G. Brown has pointed out, "what is essentially the same argument: metaphysical demonstration of a First Cause in the manner of Aristotle and identification of the First Cause with a Christian God."[5] There was, in short, no doubt in Johnson's mind that God existed and that he was the God of Christianity. But Johnson did possess considerable doubts about God's nature. "You see," as he summed up the problem for Boswell, "he must be good as well as powerful, because there is nothing to make him otherwise, and goodness of itself is preferable. Yet you have against this, what is very certain, the unhappiness of human life."[6]

Johnson conceived of God as the source of all life and as the supreme ruler of the universe, as man's "Creator, and Governour, his Father and his Judge" (Sermon 3).[7] He acknowledged with equal conviction God's omnipotence and perfect liberty. But he was more uncertain about two other traditional attributes: his goodness and his omniscience.

3

Johnson best expressed what he wanted to believe regarding God's goodness in Sermon 21. "For if he be self-existent, omnipotent, and possessed of perfect liberty; if it be impossible for him ever to err, or mistake, in what is good and fitting, and if he enjoys an infinite ability to effect, with a thought only, what shall always be for the greatest advantage, he must be originally and essentially, immutably and for ever good." Johnson saw, furthermore, ample evidence of this goodness in "the outworks of the visible creation," but he also saw the need to reconcile this goodness with the other great attribute of the Deity, namely, his justice. And this problem was for Johnson, as for all men of religious persuasion, a difficult one. How was one to reconcile divine mercy with a system of divine justice? Johnson's solution was traditional: it was to affirm the infinite goodness of God and to accept the necessity of divine judgment as the only way to insure man's obedience to the divine will. And so God was for Johnson a father who would exact punishment from his sinful son and yet grant him mercy upon signs of repentance and reformation.

Most of the time Johnson was able to live with his conception of the Deity as a rigorous but merciful judge who "will not leave his promises unfulfilled nor his threats unexecuted," but who administered a system where "every action shall at last be followed by its due consequences; we shall be treated according to our obedience or transgressions" (Sermon 10). He realized that this system of divine justice was essentially based on hope and fear, namely, the hope of reward (salvation) and the fear of punishment (damnation), but he accepted it as the only sensible basis for a moral standard of human conduct. But at other times Johnson was deeply disturbed by a sense of God as an "implacable omnipotence" who might not be merciful and who might not forgive penitent man his sins. As he made clear in Sermon 2, such a thought was appalling but real to him. "Were there not mercy with him, were he not to be reconciled after the commission of a crime; what must be the state of those, who are conscious of having once offended him? A state of gloomy melancholy, or outrageous desperation; a dismal weariness of life, and inexpressible agonies at the thought of death: for what affright or affliction could equal the horrors of that mind, which expected every moment to fall into the hands of implacable omnipotence?" This was not an idle fancy; this was not Calvinist rhetoric. It was rather the passionate imaginative vision of a devout Christian who feared not only moral anarchy but even the possibility that he could never regain divine grace and achieve salvation. It was the troubled expression of a man who admitted his own sinfulness, who sought forgiveness, but who feared he would never be granted a second chance and would never be redeemed.

Johnson was torn between what he wanted to believe and

what he feared might be true. He wanted to believe, as he remarked in Sermon 22, that "temporal punishments are the merciful admonitions of God, to avoid, by a timely change of conduct, that state in which there is no repentance, and those pains which can have no end," but he feared that much of human suffering resulted from a more capricious and indifferent source. He feared that God was not always scrupulous in the administration of justice and he feared further that man could never hope to escape from the possibility of divine punishment, even in a future state. Conversing with Boswell on this subject in 1777, Johnson, quite characteristically, hedged his response. "We have no reason to be sure," he observed, "that we shall then be no longer liable to offend against God. We do not know that even the angels are quite in a state of security; nay we know that some of them have fallen. It may, therefore, perhaps be necessary, in order to preserve both men and angels in a state of rectitude, that they should have continually before them the punishment of those who have deviated from it; but we may hope that by some other means a fall from rectitude may be prevented."[8] The moderate tone of his response, so unlike many of his stentorian outbursts on this delicate subject, struck Boswell as noteworthy and caused him to remark: "He talked to me upon this awful and delicate question in a gentle tone, and as if afraid to be decisive."

Boswell was right: Johnson was deeply uncertain on this crucial question. He was reluctant to admit that even in a future state, after man had presumably been redeemed, man could sin again and thus expect to be punished again. And this reluctance sprang ultimately from his fear that God could never be appeased, that man could never be certain he had been redeemed. Behind this carefully reasoned discourse lurked Johnson's fear that man could never escape fully the wrath of God nor enjoy fully the love of God—either in this life or the next. Johnson shuddered at this thought, shied away from what it implied about the nature of the Deity, and took solace in the insubstantial hope that by "some other means a fall from rectitude [might] be prevented." Johnson knew this hope was thin, but it was preferable to living in a constant fear of divine punishment and in the greater horror of what Johnson called "annihilation."

Johnson defined annihilation in the *Dictionary* as "the act of reducing to nothing" or "the state of being reduced to nothing."

And he most often used the word in a religious context to describe the worst possible state that man could experience after death. As he remarked to Boswell on their Scottish tour, "no wise man will be contented to die, if he thinks he is to go into a state of punishment. Nay, no wise man will be contented to die, if he thinks he is to fall into annihilation: for however unhappy any man's existence may be, he yet would rather have it, than not exist at all."[9] Death was hard enough to contemplate; damnation was even worse because of the reality of eternal pain; but annihilation was still worse because it involved the complete destruction of the human soul. And such destruction Johnson could not bear to think on, largely because of what it implied about the existence and nature of God. It implied either that God did not exist and that the universe was at the mercy of some amoral force, or that God did exist but was ultimately indifferent to the fate of fallen man. To accept either notion was to admit that man had no chance to be saved. To admit this possibility was, at least for Johnson, to affirm that life had no meaning. And this Johnson could not face without madness or despair. As a result Johnson sought to repress this disturbing conception of the Deity and to seek refuge in the traditional notion of God as a merciful judge. It was this latter view that he reaffirmed just six months before he died, when to Dr. Adams, who had suggested that God was infinitely good, Johnson replied, "that he is infinitely good, as far as the perfection of his nature will allow, I certainly believe, but it is necessary for good upon the whole, that individuals should be punished."[10] Johnson argued strongly for this conception, not because he had sufficient evidence or because he took the matter on faith, but because not to attribute such benevolence was too disturbing. "Without the most enlarged notions of an infinite and everlasting goodness in the divine nature, an impenetrable gloom must hang over every mind, and darkness over-spread the whole face of being" (Sermon 21). Here for the first time in Johnson's religious thinking we see the extent to which there were forces within him that were constantly at war with what he wanted to believe, with what he knew a good Church-of-England man ought to believe. We see the extraordinary lengths to which he went to sustain his faith because his need to believe was so great. Johnson effected the same sort of compromise when he reflected upon the problem of divine omniscience.

4

The question was in essence the problem of free will or, as it was often called in the seventeenth and eighteenth centuries, "necessity." Johnson defined free will in the *Dictionary* as "the power of directing our own actions without restraint by necessity or fate." His one citation under this definition, taken from Locke, makes clear that Johnson initially thought of this problem as more of a moral than a theological issue: "We have a power to suspend the prosecution of this or that desire; this seems to me the source of all liberty; in this seems to consist that which is improperly called freewill." But when we turn and examine the numerous definitions and citations listed under the various cognates of "necessity," we rapidly realize that the problem was also an important theological one for Johnson. For example, under "necessarily," which Johnson defined in its third meaning as "by fate; not freely," a passage from Robert South reveals Johnson's interest in this aspect of the problem: "They subjected God to the fatal chain of causes, whereas they should have resolved the necessity of all inferior events into the free determination of God himself; who executes necessarily, that which he first proposed freely." The truth is that the question for Johnson was important both for the way it affected the moral life of man and for the way it related to our conception of God.

Johnson's own position on the matter was clear: he believed in free will. He made this plain in 1769, in conversation with Boswell, who had raised the question partly out of intellectual curiosity and partly out of the desire to probe what he sensed was a vulnerable chink in Johnson's religious armor. Johnson cut short all discussion by his dogmatic assertion that "we *know* our will is free, and *there's* an end on 't."[11] But this remark did not satisfy Boswell any more than it should satisfy us; for Johnson had neither clarified nor solved the problem. He had simply stated his opinion. What Boswell rightly suspected was that Johnson himself was not as convinced of the truth of this remark as his authoritative tone might suggest. And so ten days later, in the midst of a conversation touching on a variety of religious topics, Boswell again took up this matter. He approached it from a different point of view, asking this time if we attribute "universal prescience" to the Deity must we not then believe in moral determinism? The ensuing exchange is worth quoting in full, including Boswell's observations on its significance:

> Johnson. 'Why, Sir, does not God every day see things going on without preventing them?' Boswell. 'True, Sir; but if a thing be *certainly* foreseen, it must be fixed, and cannot happen otherwise; and if we apply this consideration to the human mind, there is no free will, nor do I see how prayer can be of any avail.' He mentioned Dr. Clarke, and Bishop Bramhall on Liberty and Necessity, and bid me read South's *Sermons on Prayer;* but avoided the question which has excruciated philosophers and divines, beyond any other.[12]

Johnson again failed to make a full and coherent statement on this subject. The question he posed suggests that he was about to offer an orthodox explanation of free will by distinguishing between what God knows and what man chooses to do. This line of reasoning was familiar and traditional, and had received its most transcendent expression in *Paradise Lost,* where God absolved himself of being the cause of evil by declaring that he had given man complete freedom of moral choice. "All he could have; I made him just and right, / Sufficient to have stood though free to fall" (3:98–99). Boswell, however, was not satisfied with the implied argument and pursued the question with great rigor, concluding that free will was impossible and prayer useless in such a deterministic universe. Boswell, in short, challenged Johnson to refute the notion of determinism. And Johnson in essence capitulated when he chose to offer not his own views but instead those of three respected Anglican divines.

Of the three, Bishop Bramhall was the most noteworthy, having engaged in a famous controversy with Hobbes on this precise subject.[13] After an initial exchange, Bramhall printed in 1655 his own piece along with that of Hobbes as *A Defense of True Liberty from Antecedent and Extrinsical Necessity,* and a year later Hobbes responded in kind by publishing his critique of Bramhall's *Defense* as *The Questions Concerning Liberty, Necessity, and Chance.* Bramhall was the articulate spokesman for free will while Hobbes, of course, argued with cool precision for necessity. Johnson appears to have read the main works in question since he quotes "Bramhall against Hobbes" three times in the *Dictionary* and since he owned a complete Dublin edition of Bramhall's works. He had also continued to explore the subject, most particularly in the writings of Clarke, who in the Boyle lectures of 1705 and 1706 carried into the early eighteenth century the orthodox argument of Bramhall. But, as Chester Chapin has pointed out, there is no solid proof that Johnson himself was convinced of the truth of their arguments.[14] And the exchange quoted above supports this view as Johnson failed to give a reasoned and convincing reply to Boswell, who well knew that this behavior was uncharacteristic and who, in one of the important moments of the *Life,* took time to speculate on the origins of this unnatural reticence.

> I did not press it further, when I perceived that he was displeased, and shrunk from any abridgment of an attribute usually ascribed to the Divinity, however irreconcilable in its full extent with the grand system of moral government. His supposed orthodoxy here cramped the vigorous powers of his understanding. He was confined by a chain which early imagination and long habit made him think massy and strong, but which, had he ventured to try, he could at once have snapt asunder.[15]

Boswell's analysis was incisive and right. Johnson fell silent after his recommendation and "avoided the question," because he had not been able to answer it to his own satisfaction. He was "displeased" not because Boswell had raised the question but because he had not been able to answer it in accord with the orthodox view of free will as expressed in Article 10 of the Anglican Articles of Religion. He had looked necessity in the eye, seen its inevitable truth, and then refused to accept the implications of what he had seen. He realized that reason itself dictated acceptance of the doctrine of necessity, but he himself could not accept such a view because it demanded by definition belief in an amoral and deterministic universe. To follow the dictates of his reason meant that he must utterly abandon his conception of a benevolent God. And this Johnson could not do: he abhorred the thought of living in such a world. He had to believe that man had the power of moral choice, which, if exercised in the pursuit of good, would win him favor in the eyes of God. As he summarized the problem much later to Boswell, "all theory is against the freedom of the will; all experience for it."[16] And as Chester

Chapin has suggested, this remark may be as close as Johnson ever came to admitting the real power of Hobbes's argument.[17] Johnson may have recognized its power but he could not accept its truth. And as a result Johnson sought refuge in the harbor of Anglican orthodoxy, where he stoutly defended the existence of free will but where he continued to be haunted by the specter of determinism.

5

Although Johnson resolutely maintained his belief in the goodness, justice, and omnipotence of God, nevertheless he did not shrink from the manifest misery of human life. He recognized that the central issue in the formation of any credible theodicy was the problem of evil. And Johnson, as he made clear in his scathing review of Soame Jenyns's *Free Inquiry into the Nature and Origin of Evil* (1757), had no patience with anyone who tried to sentimentalize the pains of poverty or rationalize the existence of evil. Evil did exist; misery was real; and they both had to be faced squarely. To deny or to ignore the existence of either was to indulge in cant or, worse still, to court madness.

Johnson accepted the traditional Christian distinction between moral and physical evil. He conceived of moral evil as those acts that arise as a result of a conscious disobedience to the divine will. And he designated such acts as sins, crimes, or offenses. He thought of physical evil as all those miseries that befall man from some unknown and mysterious source, such as death, illness, pain, and war. The great exemplar of moral evil was Satan, who rebelled against the divine law and who thus brought sin into the world, while the supreme embodiment of physical evil was Job, who for inexplicable reasons was made to endure a series of terrible afflictions. And thus when Johnson reflected with Boswell on "what is very certain, the unhappiness of human life," he was thinking both of the misery that we bring upon ourselves for our failure to observe the moral laws as well as that suffering we experience for no clear reason.

Johnson attributed the pervasive unhappiness of human life not to an indifferent God but rather to man's imperfect nature and first disobedience. He absolved God of all responsibility for man's sins and put the blame squarely upon man himself. "We are informed by the Scriptures," he wrote in Sermon 5, "that God is not the Author of our present state, that when he created man, he created him for happiness; happiness indeed dependant upon his own choice, and to be preserved by his own conduct; for such must necessarily be the happiness of every resonable being; that this happiness was forfeited by a breach of the conditions to which it was annexed, and that the posterity of him that broke the covenant were involved in the consequences of his fault. Thus religion shews us that physical and moral evil entered the world together." This was the traditional Christian explanation of evil that Johnson would have learned in his catechism as a young boy and that he almost certainly would have related, as Richard Schwartz has rightly suggested, to Milton's view of evil in *Paradise Lost*.[18] Here, as in *Idler* 89, Johnson makes clear that he believes "that misery and sin were produced together," that "the depravation of human will was followed by a disorder of the harmony of nature."[19] But his own thinking on this important problem was more complex than he admitted in most of his published writings.

Of the two kinds of evil, Johnson had far less difficulty in understanding the origin of moral evil; for he believed that it clearly derived from the existence of moral choice. As he explained the matter to Boswell, "moral evil is occasioned by free will, which implies choice between good and evil."[20] And it was man's initial decision to choose to disobey God's will that brought sin and suffering into the world. Johnson never wavered from this conviction, as Lady Macleod discovered when she naively asked him if man were not naturally good, to which Johnson replied, "No, madam, no more than a wolf." Boswell, sensing a fine moment, pursued the point by asking, "Nor no woman, sir?" to which Johnson responded, "No, sir." Lady Macleod replied softly, "This is worse than Swift."[21] Although this exchange has its comic aspect, it is an accurate reflection of Johnson's conviction of man's natural depravity, as Mrs. Thrale has confirmed. "The natural depravity of mankind and remains of original sin were so fixed in Mr. Johnson's opinion," she observed, "that he was indeed a most acute observer of their effects."[22] But Johnson, unlike Swift, did not seek to rub man's nose in his baseness. He instead used the fact of human misery to give "us reason to hope for a future state of compensation, that there may be a perfect system."[23]

By this "future state of compensation," Johnson, of course,

meant belief in the Christian doctrine of immortality. He meant that man could be compensated for the suffering experienced in this life by the possibility of everlasting felicity in the life to come. He meant that man should use this life to do all he could to regain God's grace and to obtain salvation; for, as he remarked in Sermon 15, "the business of life is to work out our salvation." And thus life itself became for Johnson, as it has been for so many Christians, a trial in which he sought to purify his tainted soul and acquire redemption through obedience to the divine will, performance of good works, and expressions of faith. Johnson gave eloquent expression to his ideal when he asserted in Sermon 10 that "we are *here,* not in our *total,* nor in our *ultimate existence,* but in a state of exercise and probation, commanded to qualify ourselves, by pure hearts and virtuous actions, for the enjoyment of future felicity in the presence of God." Johnson thus rendered an imperfect system "perfect" by seeing this life as at heart an opportunity to redirect our lives according to God's will. He made human life bearable and meaningful by affirming the ultimate justice of divine providence, by expressing his "firm belief that whatever evils are suffered to befal [man] will finally contribute to his felicity" (Sermon 14). And in so doing he was able to reconcile the God of Nature with the God of the New Testament. It is no wonder then that Johnson agreed with Boswell that "the great article of Christianity [was] the revelation of immortality," and that he stated without qualification on another occasion that it was "the one solid basis of happiness."[24]

Johnson's response to the existence of physical evil, or to what he most often called misery, was more complex and less assured than his response to moral evil, largely because he was less certain about its ultimate origin. He argued, as we saw above, that such evil was a direct consequence of the primal act of disobedience, but it is clear from what he wrote elsewhere that this explanation did not entirely satisfy him. He wanted to believe that man himself was responsible for the misery that he experienced in human life, but he could never persuade himself that this was the whole truth. He was haunted throughout life by the fear that misery was inherent in life itself. As he observed in Sermon 12, "the labours of man are not only uncertain, but imperfect. If we perform what we designed, we yet do not obtain what we expected. What appeared great when we desired it, seems little when it is attained; the wish is still unsatisfied, and something always remains behind; without which, the gratification is incomplete. He that rises to greatness, finds himself in danger; he that obtains riches, perceives that he cannot gain esteem. He that is caressed, sees interest lurking under kindness; and he that hears his own praises, suspects that he is flattered. Discontent and doubt are always pursuing us. Our endeavours end without performance, and performance ends without satisfaction." Unhappiness was indeed the natural state of man; it was an ineradicable fact of human life. Unable to account for its existence and forced to acknowledge its powerful effects, Johnson turned his attention to the problem of how best to deal with misery. And his solution was a characteristic blend of psychological and religious measures.

He emphasized at the start the importance of distinguishing between real and imaginary evils, between those that truly exist and those that are the product of a restless imagination. He recognized from his own experience and from observation of others, as Richard Schwartz has put it, "the ways in which man manufactures evil, perceives it subjectively, exaggerates it, and enjoys it."[25] He realized that man brought much of his own pain upon himself by an unconscious desire to fill the vacuities of his mind and to relieve the boredom of his life. And he expressed great impatience, if not irritation, with those who permitted such imaginary pains to depress their spirits since such misery could be avoided. In *Adventurer* 111, Johnson observed that "we are often made unhappy, not by the presence of any real evil, but by the absence of some fictitious good; of something which is not required by any real want of nature, which has not in itself any power of gratification, and which neither reason nor fancy would have prompted us to wish, did we not see it in the possession of others."[26] He saw that much of our unhappiness was self-created, either because we fail to check the restless energy of the imagination or because we fail to exercise our reason upon "the real worth of that which is ardently desired." Only the rigorous and vigilant eye of reason could detect and expose such imaginary evils and thus rescue man from so much unnecessary unhappiness.

Johnson's deepest concern however, was how best to respond to the real misery of human life, to the feeling that in the words from Ecclesiastes "all was vanity and vexation of spirit."

Nowhere did he state his response more precisily than at the end of Sermon 12, where he reflected upon the "consequences the serious and religious mind may draw from the position, that all is vanity." He went on to observe: "When the present state of man is considered, when an estimate is made of his hopes, his pleasures, and his possessions; when his hopes appear to be deceitful, his labours ineffectual, his pleasures unsatisfactory, and his possessions fugitive, it is natural to wish for an abiding city, for a state more constant and permanent, of which the objects may be more proportioned to our wishes, and the enjoyments to our capacities; and from this wish it is reasonable to infer, that such a state is designed for us by that infinite wisdom, which, as it does nothing in vain, has not created minds with comprehensions never to be filled. When revelation is consulted, it appears that such a state is really promised, and that, by the contempt of worldly pleasures, it is to be obtained." Here Johnson makes clear that the only rational way to endure the radical misery of life is by placing trust in the truth of revelation and in the hope of immortality.

His response is, of course, familiar and conventional; it is the traditional Christian reply to the problem of pain. And Johnson believed in it; he found it comforting. But he also knew how inadequate it was; he knew that it could not solve the misery of life. It could only offer solace; it could only assuage temporarily the anguish of existence. And this realization deeply disturbed Johnson for what it meant about the nature of life itself as well as the notion of a divinely ordered universe. It caused him to fear that life might be meaningless and that the ruler of the universe might be indifferent. His response to these fears was characteristic: he repressed them as best he could and sought refuge in what he considered the perfection of the system. And that perfection rested upon an unqualified acceptance of the truth of revelation, which Johnson found more difficult to maintain than his own remarks, quoted earlier, might suggest. Nowhere is this difficulty more clearly manifested than in his complex response to David Hume's celebrated attack upon miracles.

6

Johnson knew little about Hume, having met him twice, and having read desultorily in his published work.[27] What Johnson did know of him he disliked intensely, considering him, as did so many other orthodox believers of his generation, "the great infidel." When, however, Boswell, who knew both men well, mentioned to Johnson in 1763 Hume's argument against belief in miracles, he received a very civil and thoughtful response.

> Why, Sir, the great difficulty of proving miracles should make us very cautious in believing them. But let us consider; although God has made Nature to operate by certain fixed laws, yet it is not unreasonable to think that he may suspend those laws, in order to establish a system highly advantageous to mankind. Now the Christian religion is a most beneficial system, as it gives us light and certainty where we were before in darkness and doubt. The miracles which prove it are attested by men who had no interest in deceiving us; but who, on the contrary, were told that they should suffer persecution, and did actually lay down their lives in confirmation of the truth of the facts which they asserted. Indeed, for some centuries the heathens did not pretend to deny the miracles; but said they were performed by the aid of evil spirits. This is a circumstance of great weight. Then, Sir, when we take the proofs derived from prophecies which have been so exactly fulfilled, we have most satisfactory evidence. Supposing a miracle possible, as to which, in my opinion, there can be no doubt, we have as strong evidence for the miracles in support of Christianity, as the nature of the thing admits.[28]

This reply is much more dispassionate and reasoned than are most of his recorded comments about Hume. Johnson is not "talking for victory" here nor trying to ridicule, as he often did, the substance of Hume's remarks. Nor does he deliver an *ad hominem* attack—he does not even mention Hume's name nor the title of his controversial piece (which is, of course, "Of Miracles," section 10 of *An Enquiry Concerning Human Understanding*)—but instead addresses the subject itself with great care. His disinterested tone confirms Donald Siebert's conviction "that Johnson must have found much of Hume's inquiry stimulating and useful—a kind of thinking to be reckoned with, certainly not rejected out of hand."[29] We feel, in short, that Johnson is trying not so much to wrestle Hume down as he is to take account of Hume's position and to state as best he can the case for revelation.

The case Johnson makes is familiar and traditional, but, as he presents it, weak and unconvincing. He is least persuasive at the start and finish of his commentary, where he is clearly responding to Hume's argument but where he fails to refute him. "The core of Hume's argument against the validity of miracles," as Charles E. Noyes has nicely summed it up, "is that the evidence against each of them is necessarily greater than the evidence for them—and we cannot, in reason, accept the lesser probability as true. It is more probable, Hume maintains, that those attesting to the miracle should be lying, or should be themselves deceived, than that the miracle should have come about."[30] Johnson is unable to establish a logical argument for the existence of miracles and is forced to fall back upon flat assertions and unsubstantiated opinions. He justifies the existence of miracles on the dubious grounds of divine need, that is, "in order to establish a system highly advantageous to mankind." And he implies that we should accept them because they are an essential part of Christianity and because Christianity "is a most beneficial system, as it gives us light and certainty where we were before in darkness and doubt." But Johnson's argument does not come close to answering Hume. It is, in fact, nothing but an opinion, nothing but an expression of what Johnson wanted to believe in order to maintain his faith in the truths of Christianity.

Johnson makes a stronger showing, however, when he argues for the validity of miracles on the traditional grounds of testimony and comparative credibility. Johnson had given much serious attention to this subject: he had examined the relevant passages in the New Testament; he had consulted biblical commentaries; he had read Grotius, Clarke, and Pearson; and he had thought carefully about the nature of testimony itself.[31] As a result of this effort, he knew what he thought on this question. "The Christian religion has very strong evidences. It, indeed, appears in some degree strange to reason; but in History we have undoubted facts, against which, in reasoning *a priori*, we have more arguments than we have for them; but then, testimony has great weight, and casts the balance."[32] And it was to the force of testimony that Johnson here appealed when he sought to establish a rational basis for faith. He trusted the original witnesses, saw no reason why they should lie, and did not consider that they might have been deceived in spite of themselves.

Although he appears at his best in this part of the commentary, nevertheless he has still not refuted the heart of Hume's argument, namely, that "no human testimony can have such force as to prove a miracle, and make it a just foundation for any such system of religion."[33] He did not refute it because he could not do so, because given Hume's precise methodology there was no way in which he could provide proof for a rational belief in the existence of miracles. All he could do was to argue that such miracles were possible—"supposing a miracle possible, as to which, in my opinion, there can be no doubt"—to make as strong a case "as the nature of the thing admits," and then to fall silent. Johnson had in fact reached the same point as Hume, the point at which it became clear that there were no rational grounds upon which to believe in miracles. But here they parted ways. Johnson's need to believe was so profound that he could not reject the evidence that appeared to support his faith while Hume's respect for intellectual integrity impelled him to pursue the implications of his argument in the following section of the *Enquiry*, entitled "Of a Particular Providence and of a Future State."

Here Hume explored the question of a divine providence in terms of his theory of cause and effect. "When we infer any particular cause from an effect, we must proportion the one to the other, and can never be allowed to ascribe to the cause any qualities, but what are exactly sufficient to produce the effect." Applying this approach to what man knows about the nature of God and the operation of divine justice, Hume substantially undercut the confidence that many of his contemporaries had in the so-called argument from design by showing the limits of what we could reasonably deduce from what we know. "Allowing, therefore, the gods to be the authors of the existence or order of the universe; it follows that they possess that precise degree of power, intelligence, and benevolence, which appears in their workmanship; but nothing farther can ever be proved."

Of far greater significance, however, was his incisive dissection of the arguments traditionally set forth for "a supreme distributive justice in the universe." If such a system exists, "I ought," Hume observed, "to expect some more particular reward of the good, and punishment of the bad, beyond the ordinary course of events." But as Hume looked about him he saw no such evidence. He admitted that divine justice might exist but it was not proven. It was a possibility, but it was not a fact that had been verified by experience. "The subject," Hume concluded, "lies entirely beyond the reach of human experience. It is useless because our knowledge of this cause being derived entirely from the course of nature, we can never, according to the rules of just reasoning, return back from the cause with any new inference, or making additions to the common and experienced course of nature, establish any principles of conduct and behavior." The implication was clear and critical: there was no reason to believe in the workings of divine justice, the doctrine of immortality, or the existence of the Christian God. There was no reason, moreover, to place much confidence in religion itself in any form. "No new fact can ever be inferred from the religious hypothesis; no event foreseen or foretold; no reward or punishment expected or dreaded, beyond what is already known by practice and observation."[34]

We do not know what Johnson thought of section 11 nor that he even read it. All we have been able to ascertain is that Johnson did read James Beattie's *Essay on Truth* (1770), one of the numerous responses to Hume's attack, and, like many of his contemporaries, thought Beattie had "confuted" Hume.[35] But as Chester Chapin has pointed out, Beattie unintentionally misrepresented some of Hume's central arguments, not the least of which were Hume's doubts about what man could know about the ultimate origins of the universe.[36] Beattie implied that Hume held that there was no "rational" cause of the universe when in fact Hume had argued that man can never know anything for certain about this cause. This confusion has created two problems with regard to Johnson. First, we do not know how to interpret Johnson's remark that Beattie had "confuted" Hume. And no new light has been shed on this matter. Second, this remark has led some critics to believe, as Chapin has put it, that "Johnson—in print at least—never comes to grips with Hume's fundamental critique of religion."[37]

Johnson believed that he had understood and had come to terms with Hume's critique, but the truth is that he had an imperfect understanding of it that prevented a full response. His remarks to Boswell quoted above make clear that Johnson understood the significance of what Hume said and of how he said it. He recognized that the careful empirical method that Hume employed to make his argument was as important as the argument itself. Many people before Hume, especially the Deists of the early eighteenth century, had denied the existence of miracles and the fulfillment of the prophecies, but no one had used the instruments sanctioned by the new science, namely, experience and observation, with such precision as to cast doubt upon the validity of the orthodox argument. Johnson also recognized that Hume's attack upon the validity of miracles was in essence an assault upon revelation and indeed, by extension, upon religion itself. Johnson knew what was at stake if Hume's argument were accepted; he knew it meant the death of traditional Christianity. And it was his clear sense of the destructive implications of Hume's critique that was principally responsible for Johnson's antipathy to Hume.

Johnson, however, did not understand that though Hume had destroyed the rational basis for belief he had not ruled out the possibility of all belief. Hume had left a way open for those who wanted to believe; in his own words, "our most holy religion is founded on *Faith*, not on reason."[38] Here he admitted that religious belief was still possible but insisted that it be founded on nonrational grounds, on faith. Whether Hume ever possessed such belief has never been satisfactorily resolved and is beyond our present concerns.[39] What matters most here is that Johnson failed to realize that Hume, while seeking to discredit the traditional bases of Christian belief, did not destroy the possibility of all religious belief.

Johnson remained blind to this possibility because neither his intellectual character nor the intellectual climate of his age permitted him to ground his belief on nonrational terms. His deep respect for reason as the ultimate standard by which to determine thought and action impelled him to establish his religious life on a solid rational basis. His quest for all the available evidence was as intense at the beginning of his life when he studied Grotius as it was at the end of his life when he made clear to Dr. Adams that he always welcomed more proof. And this habitual respect for reason was reinforced by the leading religious figures of the time, all of whom, regardless of their doctrinal differences, brought reason to bear upon matters of belief.* The effect of this combined pressure was to convince Johnson that the principal basis of belief should be rational. This conviction should have granted him considerable peace of mind but it brought him instead only intense anxiety because he was forced to realize, especially after Hume's devastating attack, the genuine limitations of reason. He realized that he had two choices: to accept the implications of Hume's argument or to acknowledge its existence but ignore it for all practical purposes. Johnson chose the latter course because to accept the former was to fall into an abyss of nonbelief and moral anarchy that Johnson feared more than anything else. Unwilling to abandon his belief and the central place that it occupied in his life, he chose once again to compromise the rational demands of his nature. This compromise was never easy but it was always necessary since it was the only way he could reconcile his intellectual self-respect with his emotional needs.

*Johnson, of course, did not hold all of these figures in equal esteem. He despised the Deists for their exclusive reliance upon reason and for their total rejection of revelation, remarking on one occasion to Boswell that "no honest man could be a Deist; for no man could be so after a fair examination of the proofs of Christianity" (*Life*, 2:8). But he was more sympathetic with a figure like Joseph Butler, who as bishop of Durham sought to reconcile the Deist God of Nature with the Christian God of Revelation. And as Basil Willey has remarked, "what distinguishes Butler from most other defenders of the faith is the unusual way in which he effects [this] identification" (Basil Willey, *The Eighteenth Century Background*, 1940; reprinted, Boston: Beacon Press, 1964, p. 77). And Johnson, according to Boswell, even used "the able and fair reasoning of Butler's *Analogy*" to dispel the "scepticism in morals and religion" that troubled the blind poet Thomas Blacklock (*Life*, 5:47). Johnson, however, had the greatest respect for Samuel Clarke because he expressed better than anyone else the rational and logical grounds for belief in the truths of the Christian faith and in the efficacy of Christian morals. Although Johnson considered Clarke unorthodox on the Trinity, nevertheless he still praised him, as James Gray has nicely put it, "as an eloquent homilist, a sound explicator of the Biblical text, and most of all as a thorough interpreter of the propitiatory sacrifice" (James Gray, *The Sermons of Samuel Johnson*, Oxford: Oxford University Press, 1972, p. 66). And William Bowles records what Johnson thought of Clarke as late as 1783: "Of Dr. Clarke he spoke with great commendation for his Universality & seemed not disposed to censure him for his Heterodoxy: he held he said the Eternity of the Son & that was being far from Heretical" (*Life*, 4:524). It was in response to such figures as these, all of whom placed great emphasis upon reason albeit in different ways, that Johnson developed his own religious belief.

Johnson felt torn between his allegiance to the religion of his youth, the sturdy Anglican faith of the seventeenth century embodied in such figures as Richard Hooker, Robert Burton, and Sir Thomas Browne, and his need to respond to the more rational theology of his own culture as represented by such individuals as Joseph Butler and Samuel Clarke. He understood the nature of Hume's attack upon Christian orthodoxy; he perceived its destructive implications; and he felt the need to refute it. But he was so much a product of what T. S. Eliot once called "the old dispensation" that he found himself largely unable to refute the new empirical arguments of the Deists and skeptics. Faced with this dilemma, he chose to reaffirm his trust in the traditional truths of the Christian faith and in the traditional way their validity was established. He was not audacious enough to make Kierkegaard's leap of faith nor imaginative enough to consider James's will to believe. He could not free himself sufficiently from the old modes of justification to establish his belief either on the validity of nonrational impulses or upon faith alone.* As a result

*It is important to note that the tradition of rational Anglicanism to which Johnson belonged was not the only Anglican tradition available to him. For starting in the 1730s, Johnson was exposed to another tradition, namely, that created by the Methodists and the Evangelicals. Members of both groups thought of themselves as rational Anglicans but differed from their more orthodox brethren in the emphasis that they placed upon the power of the divine spirit to confirm the faith of the believer and to transform his personal life. Johnson knew John Wesley and introduced him to Boswell, to whom he confided on another occasion his admiration for Wesley's sincerity and his prodigious efforts at religious reformation (*Life*, 2:123). Johnson also had high praise for the "plain and familiar manner" in which the Methodists preached (*Life*, 1:458–59). Johnson followed as well the rise of the Evangelical movement and discussed many of its tenets with his close friend Hill Boothby. He may even have written the dedication to John Lindsay's *Evangelical History of Our Lord Jesus Christ Harmonized* (*Life*, 4:549–50). But as Chester Chapin has made clear, Johnson discovered that "the difference between his own religious outlook and that of Miss Boothby was considerable and important" (Chapin, *Religious Thought*, p. 69). Johnson, in particular, could not accept the Evangelical notion of "saving faith" nor the role of the Holy Spirit in the act of "conversion." Given his "wonderful experience" of 1784 and its miraculous effect upon his religious outlook, it seems almost possible to believe that had he undergone such an experience earlier, say in the 1750s when he was most intimately involved with Miss Boothby, he might have freed himself from much of the religious anxiety that later afflicted him.

Johnson became an unwitting victim of his own rationalism, suffering acute anxiety at the persistence of doubts that could never be dispelled.

7

These doubts were a constant source of anxiety in Johnson's religious life and created in him profound spiritual fears that pertained not so much to the nature of God as to the condition of man. They pertained, above all, to the problem of salvation; they pertained to the single most important question of his life: would he be saved? Johnson knew, of course, that he would never receive an answer to this question but this fact did not make his original query any less urgent. "He owned," Boswell recorded, "that our being in an unhappy uncertainty as to our salvation, was mysterious; and said, 'Ah! we must wait till we are in another state of being, to have many things explained to us.'"[40] Intellectually he knew that he must resign himself to ignorance on this question, but emotionally he resisted such submission because so much was at stake, because he could never completely dispel his fear that he might not be saved. As a very young boy he had acquired, as we have seen, a vivid sense of hell and damnation, which had deepened as the years passed. When asked six months before he died by his old friend Dr. Adams what he meant by damnation, Johnson replied with great passion, "Sent to Hell, Sir, and punished everlastingly."[41] And so the great aim of his life became to work out his salvation as best he could, but it was an undertaking that consistently filled Johnson with terrible fear. As Mrs. Thrale shrewdly observed, "his fears of his own salvation were excessive: his truly tolerant spirit, and Christian charity, which *hopeth all things,* and *believeth all things,* made him rely securely on the safety of his friends, while his earnest aspiration after a blessed immortality made him cautious of his own steps, and timorous concerning their consequences. He knew how much he had been given, and filled his mind with fancies of how much would be required, till his impressed imagination was often disturbed by them, and his health suffered from the sensibility of his too tender conscience: a real Christian is *so* apt to find his task above his power of performance!"[42]

Related to this general question regarding his possible salvation were two more particular concerns. First, as he remarked in a meditation of 1760, "what shall I do to be saved?"[43] This was, of course, not the real question; for Johnson knew full well what he must do to be redeemed. He knew that he must obey God's laws, must repent when he had sinned, and must at all times pray for divine guidance and grace. As he observed succinctly in Sermon 14, "trust in God, that trust to which perfect peace is promised, is to be obtained only by repentance, obedience, and supplication." The real question concerned not what should be done but what *could* be done; it concerned not a failure of knowledge but a failure of will. What troubled Johnson was not ignorance of what was required but fear that he could never achieve sufficient self-mastery to do what was necessary. He sought, for example, to obey both the letter and the spirit of Christian law by making "the concerns of eternity the governing principles of [his life]," but he found it difficult to reconcile this religious ideal with his passionate worldly nature.[44] As Maurice Quinlan has rightly observed, Johnson's chief religious conflict was "not between faith and doubt. It was a struggle, common enough in deeply pious persons, between a dedication to spiritual values and the attractions of the world."[45] Convinced that he had a fundamental religious responsibility to make the most of the time and talents granted to him, Johnson lamented at almost every point that he had not been able to do more. At Easter 1758, Johnson, in spite of all that he had accomplished in the preceding years, wrote: "Grant me thy Holy Spirit, that after all my lapses I may now continue stedfast in obedience, that after long habits of negligence and sin, I may at last work out my salvation with diligence and constancy, purify my thoughts from pollutions, and fix my affections on things eternal."[46] Implicit in this prayer is Johnson's fear that he may never be able to obey the divine will with the rigor that he would like.

He possessed much the same fear about repentance. He argued for repentance; he explained its nature; and he set down in Sermons 2 and 10 how it might best be achieved.[47] But few men have written more intelligently and more sympathetically about the various ways in which man tries to rationalize deferment of this critical step. Johnson noted in Sermon 10 that "the far greater part of mankind deceive themselves, by willing negligence, by refusing to think on their real state, lest such thoughts should trouble their quiet, or interrupt their pursuits." And he went on to describe how easy it was for man "to abstract the thoughts from things spiritual," to practice "the art . . . of putting far from us . . . the hour of death and the day of account," to procrastinate "amendment in hopes of better opportunities in future time," and to believe with certainty "that the grace, without which no man can correct his own corruption, when it has been offered and refused, will be offered again."

Johnson thus clearly understood what must be done and what must be overcome in order for man to experience true repentance and to enact true reformation. It was not enough, however, to know what must be done; it was necessary to do it. And it was Johnson's acute sense of the inevitable discrepancy between intention and enactment, between promise and performance, that made him so anxious about his own spiritual condition. Once again no one has expressed better than Mrs. Thrale the way in which Johnson's struggle to render himself worthy of salvation "kept him in constant anxiety."

> "No one had however higher notions of the hard task of true Christianity than Johnson, whose daily terror lest he had not done enough, originated in piety, but ended in little less than disease. Reasonable with regard to others, he had formed vain hopes of performing impossibilities himself; and finding his good works ever below his desires and intent, filled his imagination with fears that he should never obtain forgiveness for omissions of duty and criminal waste of time. These ideas kept him in constant anxiety concerning his salvation; and the vehement petitions he perpetually made for a longer continuance on earth, were doubtless the cause of his so prolonged existence.[48]

The second particular concern that grew out of Johnson's general question regarding his salvation was: how could he be sure that he had fulfilled the conditions for salvation? His intellect told him that he could never achieve this certainty but his heart demanded an answer all the same. Reason, as Imlac had observed, could not explain what it had not dictated, but it also could not suppress, as Johnson himself realized, what the soul desired to know. And the great desire of Johnson's soul was to know whether he had done enough to be saved. He knew, as we have seen, that obedience and repentance were the principal requisite conditions for salvation, but he also knew that no true believer could ever be certain that he had satisfactorily met these terms. He revealed the depth of this conviction in a conversation with Mrs. Knowles, who had argued that "the righteous shall have *hope* in his [Christ's] death," to which Johnson replied, "But what man can say that his obedience has been such, as he would approve of in another, or even in himself upon close examination, or that his repentance has not been such as to require being repented of? No man can be sure that his obedience and repentance will obtain salvation."[49]

Johnson was psychologically incapable of believing that he could ever have been obedient or penitent enought to merit redemption. Part of this deeply rooted reluctance sprang from his fear of spiritual presumption and part of it sprang from his sense of his own unworthiness and sinfulness. Although the causes of this reluctance are complex, nevertheless its effect was clear. It created in him an additional spiritual anxiety that remained with him until the very end. Just nine months before he died, Johnson discussed this same subject with Mrs. Thrale. "Goodness," he remarked, "always wishing to be better, and imputing every deficience to criminal negligence, and every fault to voluntary corruption, never dares to suppose the conditions of forgiveness fulfilled, nor what is wanting in the crime supplied by Penitence. This is the state of the best, but what must be the condition of him whose heart will not suffer him to rank himself among the best, or among the good, such must be his dread of the approaching trial, as will leave him little attention to the opinion of those whom he is leaving for ever, and the serenity that is not felt, it can be no virtue to feign."[50] Johnson never considered himself among "the best" nor even permitted himself to acknowledge that he had done as well as he could. He was always haunted by what he had failed to do, by what he had left undone.

8

This spiritual anxiety manifested itself in Johnson's everyday life as an ongoing battle against melancholy, against those periods of depression when Johnson would be troubled by guilt and "vain imaginations," by "scruples" and terrors. Such moments occurred with great frequency throughout his life, and though he usually managed to overcome them relatively quickly through diversion and involvement in other activities, they were never entirely dispelled. Like the fog that seems to lie offshore and threatens to return on even the sunniest of days, these dark moods could recur at any time. Johnson never felt totally free from them. They always lurked in his mind as something that must be controlled as best he could.

Johnson first became fascinated with this affliction as a result of his terrible breakdown of 1730, during which he made his first known inquiry into the origin of this crippling malady. He wrote, as may be remembered, an account of his case in Latin and presented it to Dr. Swinfen, his godfather and the local physician in Lichfield.[51] Dr. Swinfen was so impressed by the intelligence of the analysis that, much to Johnson's horror, he broke professional confidence and discussed the case in public. Unfortunately, neither Johnson's original report nor a later summary of its substance has been preserved so we do not know what Johnson's thoughts were on the matter. But it would not be surprising if it anticipated in a general way what he later came to believe regarding the origin of his melancholy as well as what he might have included in a projected history of this affliction, which he mentioned in 1769 but which he never completed.[52]

Johnson had two basic explanations for the melancholy that he suffered throughout his life. First, he believed that to a large extent he had inherited this "vile" affliction from his father, whom he described to Mrs. Thrale as "wrong-headed, positive, and afflicted with melancholy."[53] Although he must have recognized the limitations of this view, his assertion that his father's "vile melancholy . . . made him mad all his life, at least not sober" reflects the degree to which he did hold his father responsible.[54] As he grew older, however, Johnson developed another theory, largely based on his own experience and from his own reading in the subject—in Robert Burton's *Anatomy* and in Dr. George Cheyne's *The English Malady,* to name two studies that he praised highly.[55] He came to believe that his melancholy derived from the interaction of indolence and the imagination; it arose from the operation of the imagination upon an idle and vapid mind. Johnson knew that he was unusually susceptible to idleness, and remarked to Boswell on one occasion that "he always felt an inclination to do nothing."[56] And he developed such guilt over this failing that late in his life he designated it as his principal flaw.

"My reigning sin, to which perhaps many others are appendent, is waste of time, and general sluggishness, to which I am always inclined and in part of my life have been almost compelled by morbid melancholy and disturbance of mind. Melancholy has had in me its paroxisms and remissions, but I have not improved the intervals, nor sufficiently resisted my natural inclination, or sickly habits."[57] He believed, in short, that he suffered from chronic laziness and that this weakness had brought on moments of instability and depression. But he had not made clear, as W. B. C. Watkins has put it, how "the Castle of Indolence is merely a way station to the Cave of Despair."[58]

Johnson's account of the origin of his melancholy remained incomplete and unsatisfactory until he obtained a fuller understanding of the power of the imagination. It was not until his midforties, not until after the death of his wife, Tetty, in 1752, that he recognized the dangerous and destructive role that the imagination played in man's quest for spiritual happiness. From his use of this word in his diaries, it is clear that he thought of the imagination in two distinct but related ways. First, it was the word he tended to use to describe the sexual fantasies that he experienced in the years following Tetty's death. Possessed of a strong sexual drive, as W. J. Bate has recently shown, Johnson found it difficult to repress these feelings and experienced much guilt at their unwanted appearance.[59] Six weeks after Tetty died he wrote the following prayer: "And now, O Lord, release me from my sorrow, fill me with just hopes, true faith, and holy consolations, and enable me to do my duty in that state of life to which Thou has been pleased to call me, without disturbance from fruitless grief, or tumultuous imaginations."[60] Second, Johnson also used the word to refer to his fear of mental instability, often in connection with such phrases as "vain terrours." This usage was most common in the 1760s, when Johnson underwent a prolonged religious crisis. Here is a passage excerpted from his Easter prayer of 1764: "Deliver me from habitual wickedness, and idleness, enable me to purify my thoughts, to use the faculties which thou has given me with honest diligence, and to regulate my life by thy holy word. . . . Deliver me from the distresses of vain terrour and enable me by thy Grace to will and to do what may please thee."[61]

From these two different but related uses, it is clear that in Johnson's mind the imagination was related to sin and sensuality, to emotional instability and madness. It was related directly to all those ills of the body and the soul that kept man from reflecting on his true concerns, namely, his quest for salvation. Johnson made this more general point explicit in a prayer he wrote on March 31, 1771. "O Lord God, in whose hand are the wills and affections of man, kindle in my mind holy desires, and repress sinful and corrupt imaginations. Enable me to love thy commandments, and to desire thy promises; let me by thy protection and influence so pass through things temporal, as finally not to lose the things eternal."[62] And thus the imagination became for Johnson not only the enemy of reason but the antagonist of faith.

It became the principal antagonist of Johnson's faith because it alone possessed the power to disorder and to render meaningless Johnson's effort to make his faith the center of his life. (Is not this the reason why he most often refers to the imagination as "tumultuous" or "vain"?) It alone had sufficient force to divert his mind from the concerns of eternity and sufficient appeal to fix his attention on the more immediate but ephemeral pleasures of this life. What Johnson never fully realized, however, was that his frequent fits of depression were rarely the result of the imagination at work upon a vacant mind but rather the result of the imagination operating upon a consciousness haunted by religious fears. He never fully grasped that the reason he considered indolence his "reigning sin" and possessed a "horror or solitude" was because it was in such listless and lonely moods that he was most apt to reflect on his uncertain spiritual condition. He would never have been troubled by his natural indolence, his sexual fantasies, and his unruly imagination if he had not considered them hostile to the great business of life. It was his preoccupation, if not his obsession, with the disparity that inevitably developed between his religious ideals and his own imperfect conduct that produced the terrible melancholy he experienced throughout his life.

Johnson thus suffered from a kind of religious melancholy that William James has shrewdly analyzed in his discussion of the distinction between "once-born" and "twice-born" souls in *The Varieties of Religious Experience*.[63] The difference in type depends upon one's conception of God as well as one's response to the problem of evil and the reality of human suffering. The "once-born," according to James, are naive optimists who see God as the embodiment of kindness, beauty, and truth and who are largely untroubled by the existence of evil and the pain of suffering. They acknowledge the existence of such problems but feel sure that they can be solved. "They see God," writes James quoting John Henry Newman, "not as a strict Judge, nor as a glorious Potentate, but as the animating Spirit of a beautiful, harmonious world, beneficent and kind, Merciful as well as Pure. The same characters generally have no metaphysical tendencies: they do not look back into themselves. Hence they are not distressed by their own imperfections: yet it would be absurd to call them self-righteous. . . . Of human sin they know perhaps little in their own hearts and not very much in the world; and human suffering does but melt them to tenderness. Thus when they approach God, no inward disturbance ensues." The "twice-born," James goes on to show, are pessimists who see God as a merciful but exacting judge and who conceive of evil as an inextricable part of human nature "which no alteration of the environment, or any superficial rearrangement of the inner self, can cure, and which requires a supernatural remedy." But the degree of the pessimism "all depends . . . on how sensitive the soul may become to discords." The depth of the pessimism depends on one's temperament, and in particular on one's reaction to the observable misery of life and to the fact of death. But the nadir of pessimism is reached only when the person becomes the "prey of a pathological melancholy." In this state, a person is forced in spite of himself to ignore all that is good and true and to become obsessed by what is bad and false. Such a state is characterized by "an incapability for joy" and "a positive and active anguish" that sometimes takes on "the quality of loathing; sometimes that of irrational exasperation; or again of self-mistrust and despair." Although James himself admits that "most are mixed cases" and warns that we should not treat his classification with too much respect, nevertheless his description of "twice-born" man resembles Johnson in many, though not in all, respects. Had James known Johnson's religious meditations, he might well have included some of them to stand alongside those he selected from Tolstoi and Bunyan to illustrate his point.

That Johnson was a pessimist, by James's standard or by any other, is indisputable. He had always thought of God as a strict judge before whom he would stand in fear and trembling to learn if he were to be damned or saved. He had always believed that evil was an ineradicable part of human life, which could be contained and mitigated but never rooted out and destroyed. And Johnson had always been especially sensitive to the pain of human life, to that cycle of expectation and disappointment that had conditioned him to see life as "a state in which much is to be endured and little to be enjoyed." But Johnson never experienced despair for any sustained period of time, as William Cowper did, because he never finally lost his faith. He never surrendered his hope for a happy futurity nor his trust in a divinely ordered universe. And he never lost his faith, not because of its inherent strength, but because of his profound need to believe that life had meaning and because of his passionate pursuit of piety to render himself worthy of redemption.

3

The Pursuit of Piety

> *Religion, of which the rewards are distant, and which is animated only by Faith and Hope, will glide by degrees out of the mind, unless it be invigorated and reimpressed by external ordinances, by stated calls to worship, and the salutary influence of example.*
>
> Johnson, *Lives of the Poets*

Johnson turned to religious devotion as the principal means to relieve his guilt at his failure to make his faith the center of his life. Torn between his desire to live in strict accord with this Christian standard and his realization that he could not do so, Johnson experienced lacerating guilt that could be appeased only by a renewed commitment to this standard through various devotional measures, some of which were prescribed by the Church and some of which were of his own invention. Taken together, they constitute a moving testament to Johnson's spiritual anxiety as well as to his extraordinary piety.

In the *Dictionary* Johnson gave five definitions of devotion: (1) the state of being consecrated or dedicated; (2) piety, acts of religion; (3) acts of external worship; (4) prayer; and (5) the state of mind under a strong sense of dependence upon God. From this listing, it is clear that Johnson thought of devotion in two different but related ways. First, it meant to him any of a variety of actions by which man rededicated himself to obeying the will of God. It involved acts of public worship performed at church, such as Holy Communion, as well as more private acts that could be done anywhere, such as personal meditation. Second, it meant an attitude of mind and heart that sought to dispose man to think of his true relationship with God. It involved the conscious directing of the mind to man's uncertain spiritual condition with the fervent hope that he would recommit himself to the pursuit of the Christian ideal. It must have been with both of these notions in mind that Johnson chose the following quotation from Law to illustrate the meaning of the fifth definition listed above: "Devotion may be considered either as an exercise of publick or private prayers at set times and occasions, or as a temper of the mind, a state and disposition of the heart, which is rightly affected with such exercises."

Devotion meant to Johnson, then, all the efforts, public or private, that a Christian makes to discharge his duty to God. And in all cases and for all men that duty was the same, namely, to confess one's sins and to seek God's grace. The aim of religious devotion was to create true humility and lasting piety. And it was only through such devotional measures that man could once again make religion the center of his life and the basis of his conduct. "The great art therefore of piety, and the end for which all the rites of religion seem to be instituted," Johnson observed in *Rambler* 7, "is the perpetual renovation of the motives to virtue, by a voluntary employment of our mind in the contemplation of its excellence, its importance, and its necessity, which, in proportion as they are more frequently and more willingly revolved, gain a more forcible and permanent influence, 'till in time they become the reigning ideas, the standing principles of actions and the test by which every thing proposed to the judgment is rejected or approved."

Johnson practiced so intensely the devotional measures that he preached that he was celebrated in his own time as a great exemplar of religious piety. Close friends like Mrs. Thrale could attest to the emotional depth of this commitment. "The piety of Dr. Johnson was exemplary and edifying: he was punctiliously exact to perform every public duty enjoined by the church, and his spirit of devotion had an energy that affected all who ever saw him pray in private. The coldest and most languid hearers of the word must have felt themselves animated by his manner of reading the holy scriptures."[1] And this same point was made again and again in almost all of the biographical accounts and memorials that appeared in such quick succession after his death.[2] Johnson, in fact, became such a model of piety that when the Reverend George Strahan came to edit and publish the private journals that became known as *The Prayers and Meditations*, he tried to strike out various passages that revealed some of Johnson's religious scruples and that thus undercut his image of Christian piety. (For example, he attempled to cross out "scrupulis obsistendum" in the meditation of April 6, 1777.[3]) And even Boswell, who tried so hard to provide a balanced portrait of Johnson, feared that he might tarnish Johnson's reputation as a pious man by his account of Johnson's death.[4]

2

The origin of this piety lay in the religious discipline to which he was exposed as a young child and in the devotional program set forth in the second half of Law's *Serious Call* that he encountered at Oxford. His mother, as Johnson himself recorded in the "Annals," initiated this discipline by forcing him to memorize prayers and learn his catechism as a young boy of three or four. Blessed with an extraordinary memory, Johnson found these exercises easy and delighted in the speed with which he could master them. It is from this time that we can date the start of his lifelong habit of quoting long passages from the *Book of Common Prayer* and the Bible. She continued to supervise her son's religious education, as Boswell recorded it, "with assiduity, but, in his [Johnson's] opinion, not with judgment." What Johnson seems to have had in mind was his enforced reading of *The Whole Duty of Man,* "from a great part of which I could derive no instruction."[5]

Although Johnson claimed he derived little benefit from this book, his remark should not serve to discredit his mother or the book. Her choice was not original—it was in fact totally conventional—but it was sensible and understandable since *The Whole Duty of Man* was the most popular conduct book of the age. Published anonymously in 1658, it had been required reading for Swift and Defoe just as it was now for Johnson and other members of his generation. Most of its appeal arose from its simple style, its lucid form, and its didactic content. It had been written "in a plain and familiar way for the use of all, but especially the meanest reader." It was avowedly low brow and aimed at securing as large an audience as it could. Its structure was transparent. It was divided into seventeen chapters, "one whereof being read every Lord's Day, the whole may be read over thrice in the year." And the moral purpose of the book was unmistakable. It was designed to define the particular duties that each Christian should perform to purify his soul. Some of the chapters were on particular sacred obligations, such as chapters three ("Of the Lord's Supper") and five ("Of Worship due to God's Name"), but most of them related to more secular duties, though treated in a moral manner, such as chapters seven ("Of Contentedness") and eight ("Of Temperance"). It was, in short, just the kind of book that a devout and well-intentioned mother like Sarah Johnson would give to her son.

Though Johnson was undoubtedly bored by much of its moralizing, he was certainly more influenced by this book than he realized at the time. He may never have read it through, but he did dip into it sporadically for the rest of his life, noting as late as 1781 that he had "read the first Sunday in the Duty of Man, in which I had till then only looked by compulsion or by chance."[6] It proved to be the first of what were to be a long line of books on religious subjects that he was constantly picking up and studying, from Grotius's *De Veritate Religionis Christi* to the long list of books that he set down in his private journal just six weeks before he died.[7] From his exposure to this influential work, furthermore, Johnson may have first acquired his conviction of the value of a disciplined, if not ritualized, approach to religious devotion. The instruction to read one chapter each Sunday and thus the whole book three times a year cannot help but remind us of his later attempts to read predetermined amounts of the New Testament each day and the entire Bible once each year. And finally, the subject matter of this work would have appealed to the moralist in Johnson. He might have been indifferent to the chapter on theft, but it is hard to believe he would have been unresponsive to the chapter on the need for temperance in sleep, which turns into a meditation on sloth. Each of these chapters anticipates in approach, tone, and theme Johnson's periodical essays and in some ways his sermons. This seminal work clearly sowed the seeds of his piety.

Johnson might well have lost his early devotional habits had they not been reinforced by his reading of Law's *Serious Call*. I have already discussed the formative influence of this book, but I must return to it now in order to define its effect upon Johnson's attitude toward religious discipline. To start, its most general effect was to intensify the serious attitude toward devotion that had been begun by Johnson's mother and that had continued in his early religious training. *A Serious Call* appealed directly to the self-confessed but struggling Christian who, like Johnson, sought to mend his ways and to live a more disciplined religious life. Law was also able to define, as his remark quoted in the *Dictionary* makes clear, the meaning of devotion with a force and clarity that Johnson could not have otherwise known. "Devotion," Law wrote on the first page of his treatise, "signifies a life given, or devoted to God." And Law goes on to argue with great passion: "He, therefore, is the devout man, who lives no longer to his own will, or the way and spirit of the world, but to the sole will of God; who considers God in everything, who serves God in everything, who makes all the parts of his common life parts of piety, by doing everything in the Name of God, and under such rules as are conformable to His glory." Such conviction was impressive in itself but became even more compelling when Law expressed complete faith in man's ability to attain this ideal. Law believed that the only hindrance to this realization was not man's innate sinfulness but his lack of desire and of proper discipline. "For whenever we fully intend it," he observed, "it is as possible to conform to all this regularity of life, as it is possible for a man to observe times of prayer. So that the fault does not lie here, that we desire to be good and perfect, but through the weakness of our nature fall short of it; but it is, because we have not piety enough to intend to be as good as we can, or to please God in all the actions of our life. This we see is plainly the case of him that spends his time in sports when he should be at Church; it is not his want of power, but his want of intention or desire to be there."[8] Man thus possessed the ability to effect this reformation, if he so desired, by engaging in a rigorous process of daily devotion.

Law devoted the second half of his work, from chapter fourteen to twenty-four, to the specific acts of devotion that should be practiced. In particular, he took up prayer and prescribed the hours during the day when one should pray—6 a.m., 9 a.m., noon, 3 p.m., 6 p.m., and before bed—as well as the subjects of each of those prayers—thanksgiving to God, humility, universal love, resignation to the divine will, examination and confession of sins, and reflection on death, respectively. He argued, furthermore, for the need of each man to adapt his prayers to "the differences of our state and the differences of our hearts." Man must adapt his prayers to the different physical and psychological states that he experiences each day. "Now by thus watching and attending to the present state of our hearts, and suiting some of our petitions exactly to their wants," Law concluded, "we shall not only be well acquainted with the disorders of our souls, but also be well exercised in the method of curing them."[9]

What Law recommended Johnson took to heart and practiced in his own erratic way for the rest of his life. He was never able to imitate the precise pattern of prayer that Law had set forth, but his habit of composing prayers, usually late at night just before he went to bed and usually using his own personal circumstances as a stimulus, undoubtedly derived in large part from this powerful example. And, as we will see in greater detail later on, the subjects of his own meditations bore a close resemblance to those of Law. He could not discipline himself to take up separate topics at separate times but tried instead at the end of the day to cover in one session all that Law had urged be limited to set times. Though Johnson often found this ascetic ideal incompatible with his own nature, he absorbed a great deal of it and used it as a standard by which to exhort himself to a purer spiritual life.

Finally, Johnson could not help but be struck by Law's faith in the pursuit of this ideal as the source of the greatest possible happiness that man could know on earth. While Law did admit that the asceticism and self-denial inherent in this ideal might create "scrupulous anxiety," nevertheless he believed that its real value was that it enabled man "to subdue, and root out of his mind, all those passions of pride, envy, and ambition . . . [that] are the causes of all the disquiets and vexations of human life." "So true is it," he concluded, "that the more we live by the rules of religion, the more peaceful and happy do we render our lives."[10]

The ultimate effect, then, of *A Serious Call* was to impress upon Johnson the importance of religious devotion in theory and to demonstrate how to implement that theory in practice. He saw how critical such discipline was to moderate the passions, to resist worldly temptations, and to make religion central to our daily life. "If our common life is not a common course of humility, self-denial, renunciation of the world, poverty of spirit, and heavenly affection, we do not live the lives of Christians."[11] Such was the devotional ideal that Johnson in large part took on as his own.

3

Johnson's own devotional practices fall into two categories. In the first were all those external acts of worship, such as attendance at church, celebration of the Eucharist, and the observation of certain holy days. All of these actions were rooted in ecclesiastical tradition, sanctioned by the Church, and dutifully observed by the devout Christian. In the second category were all those internal acts of piety, such as private prayer and meditation on days not necessarily sanctified by the Church but still important to the given individual. Johnson undertook all of these actions not simply in response to ecclesiastical authority but as a result of spiritual need. Johnson considered both kinds of devotion important but found the former more difficult to sustain than the latter. Guilt-ridden by his failure to follow practices established by the Church itself, he frequently depended on his own private meditations to renew his spiritual commitment.

4

Of all the possible external acts of worship, there was none upon which Johnson placed greater importance than attendance at church. He considered it a moral obligation, which he tried throughout his life to honor but which he never managed to perform to his satisfaction. As a result, one of the most frequent resolves of his private diaries was to go to church, if not on Sundays, then, by way of compensation, during the week. (There is, for example, mention of such resolves in 1755, 1760, 1761, 1764, 1766, 1777, and 1781.) But these resolutions had little or no effect. "Whenever I miss church on a Sunday," Johnson told Boswell, "I resolve to go another day. But I do not always do it."[12]

Johnson himself said that he had acquired this habit in boyhood when, owing to a repair then being made to Saint Mary's in Lichfield, he was instructed to attend another church but disobeyed this parental order and went to play in the fields instead. He admitted that this pattern continued for five years and to it he attributed his lifelong reluctance to attend regular worship. "This habit continued till my fourteenth year; and still I find a great reluctance to go to church."[13] The reason he gave at this time for his truancy was his poor eyesight, but as he grew older he found other excuses—his poor hearing and the mediocrity of the sermons.

Deprived of satisfying participation in the service itself, he preferred to stay at home where he could read the lessons and collects for the day as well as reflect and pray in complete peace. But in spite of this alternative and in spite of the real fervor that he brought to the private devotions, Johnson never convinced himself that they were a proper substitute. He still experienced guilt at his failure to get to church and to perform the acts of worship that he thought were proper for the true Christian. As late as 1777 he wrote, "I have this year omitted church on most Sundays, intending to supply the deficience in the week. So that I owe twelve attendances on worship." He recognized the destructiveness of such guilt when he added, "I will make no more such superstitious stipulations which entangle the mind with unbidden obligations." Just four years later, he noted: "More frequent attendance on publick Worship. Participation of the Sacrament at least three times a year."[14] He saw the vicious cycle of guilt in which he was trapped, but he could not escape it.

5

Johnson's absence from church prevented him from performing properly two duties, namely to pray and to take Holy Communion. His guilt derived largely from his failure to perform these duties. Johnson was partially able to relieve his guilt by engaging in prayer at home, of which more will be said later. But no such alternative was available to him with regard to the celebration of the Eucharist. And Johnson considered participation in this sacrament to be, along with attendance at church, one of the two principal public duties of a practicing Christian. In one of the two sermons that he wrote on this subject, Johnson defined the Eucharist as "a solemn ratification of a covenant renewed; by which, after having alienated ourselves from Christ by sin, we are restored, upon our repentance and reformation, to pardon and favour, and the certain hopes of everlasting life" (Sermon 9). He thus conceived of Communion as one of the most important means by which man sought to regain divine grace. It was the solemn symbolic expression of faith in the essential truth of Christ's mission; and its purpose was to commemorate the death of Christ, to reaffirm faith in his merits, and to inspire adherence to his religion. Johnson believed that anyone who took Communion should be a self-confessed Christian and should be willing to submit himself to continual and rigorous self-examination. "The terms, upon which we are to hope for any benefits from the merits of Christ, are faith, repentance, and subsequent obedience. These are therefore the three chief and general heads of examination" (Sermon 9). Johnson furthermore was critical of those Christians who felt they were either too unworthy or never would be worthy enough to take Communion. Such people were foolish or overly scrupulous since in Johnson's view it was not "the will of God, that any should perish, but that all should repent, and be saved" (Sermon 22). He was firmly convinced, as he went on to make clear, that he who desired to be saved could be; for "he that has eaten and drunk unworthily may enter into salvation, by repentance and amendment."

Johnson's own participation in the Eucharist was as erratic as his attendance at church. He took Communion as often as he could, especially during Lent and Easter, but he never did so with any regularity. Though negligent in his practice, Johnson sought to make up for this lapse in duty by keeping himself prepared as a worthy potential communicant. Such preparation, as he declared in Sermon 22, was only possible if it were based on self-examination, perusal of the writings of piety, and prayer. These endeavors could be undertaken alone and at home, and while never equal to taking the Sacrament at church, they still managed to preserve its essential spirit. Johnson, then, increasingly tended to perform in the privacy of his house what most people enacted in a regular public service. Such was also his practice regarding the observation of holy days.

6

Johnson consistently maintained that the observation of holy days was an important duty for the devout Christian and regretted the tendency of the Scots to ignore them. He believed, as he remarked to Boswell, that "the holidays observed by our church are of great use in religion." That use was primarily commemorative as he made clear to a Quaker who queried the Anglican practice of observing such days. "The Church," Johnson replied, "does not superstitiously observe days, merely as days, but as memorials of important facts. Christmas might be kept as well upon one day of the year as another; but there should be a stated day for commemorating the birth of our Saviour, because there is danger that what may be done on anyday, will be neglected."[15] Johnson thus took this matter seriously and even made notations in Boswell's copy of Robert Nelson's *Companion for the Festivals and Fasts of the Church of England,* the most authoritative and popular book on the subject at the time.[16]

But Johnson's practice fell far short of his principle. Although he observed some of the holy days with great care, nevertheless he was very negligent in observing other significant days of the ecclesiastical calendar. There is, for example, no mention in his private journals of the Christmas season—of Advent, Christmas, or Epiphany. One could well imagine that Johnson might have used one of these sacred days as an inspiration to rededicate himself to the Christian life, but such is not the case. The only holidays that are so observed are Lent and Easter. (There are prayers and meditations on Easter on a fairly regular basis from 1753 to the end of his life, becoming almost annual from the 1760s.)

What Johnson tended to do instead was to use days that had a particular meaning for him as a stimulus to review his past life and to make new resolves. Such days were New Year's Day, the day Tetty died (March 28), and his own birthday (September 18). On these days, Johnson conducted a rigorous self-examination, which usually consisted of a comparison of what he had set out to do with what he had failed to accomplish, after which he listed a series of resolves to amend his life. Some of this review related to sacred matters, to his failure to read the Bible through during the year, but most of it pertained to secular things, to reading projects that he had failed to complete and to habits of mind that he had been unable to control. The effect of this practice was to make Johnson's religious discipline an extremely intense and private affair. Although he affirmed the importance of public acts of worship, nevertheless his most heartfelt acts of devotion were those related to the study of religion and to prayer.

7

Although Johnson resolved on a number of occasions to study religion and to read books of divinity, nevertheless he never formally studied religion. But he did spend more time reading religion than he did any other single subject except literature.

None of this reading was done in a systematic way, that is, chronologically or topically, but rather as Johnson read most things, as they appeared and caught his interest. He acquired this habit early when he had dipped into *The Whole Duty of Man* and wrestled with Grotius's *De Veritate Religionis Christi.* And he kept it for the rest of his life. It was the force of this habit that had compelled him to pick up William Law, to peruse Thomas à Kempis, to read Samuel Ogden on prayer on his Scottish tour, and to immerse himself in the Church Fathers in the last six months of his life. Much of this reading was undertaken as an act of intellectual self-discipline, but most of it was inspired by Johnson's desire to become a better Christian. The true motivation was spiritual and not intellectual, though each tended to nourish the other, as his prayer on the study of religion makes clear. "Almighty God, our heavenly Father, without whose help, labour is useless, without whose light search is vain, invigorate my studies and direct my enquiries, that I may by due diligence and right discernment establish myself and others in thy holy Faith. Take not, O Lord, thy Holy Spirit from me, let not evil thoughts have dominion in my mind. Let me not linger in ignorance and doubt, but enlighten, and support me for the sake of Jesus Christ our Lord. Amen."[17]

When approached from this perspective, Johnson's reading takes on a clearer purpose than it otherwise might. We can see that Johnson conceived of this work as an important part of his religious discipline, as a deliberate means to increase his piety. And most of this reading fell into one of five distinct areas: the Bible, the *Book of Common Prayer,* the Church Fathers, the seventeenth-century English Protestant divines, and the eighteenth-century Anglicans.

8

The most important of these works to Johnson was, of course, the Bible. He read it throughout his life, knew large parts of it by heart, and studied it carefully with commentaries.[18] It was, along with the *Book of Common Prayer,* the one book to which he was always returning. He was always making new plans to read a portion of the Bible each day—and the entire text within the year. The first mention of such a plan occurred in 1755, when Johnson resolved "to read the Scriptures methodically with such helps as are at hand" and similar resolves appear in each succeeding year until 1772, when Johnson admitted that "at last, in my sixty third year, I have attained to know, even thus hastily, confusedly, and imperfectly, what my Bible contains."[19] But Johnson did not rest content there; he set himself to reread it but in a new language. In 1777, he decided "to read the whole Bible in some language before Easter," and in 1784, just three months before he died, he noted simply "to study the Bible."

Although Johnson did succeed in knowing the Bible as a whole, he returned more often to the Pentateuch, to the Wisdom books, and to the New Testament. Of these, Johnson preferred the New Testament because it spoke most directly to what concerned him most. As fascinating as the early history of the Jewish people was, and as moving as Psalms and Proverbs were, Johnson's deepest interests lay in the meaning of Christ's life, in the evidences for the truth of Christianity, and in the historical evolution of the early Church. Although Johnson demonstrated little interest in the well-known events of Christ's life—the Nativity, Baptism, sojourn in the wilderness, or early ministry—he was passionately interested in the meaning of Christ's death and resurrection. Convinced, furthermore, that the revelation of immortality was the central belief of Christianity, he rarely passed up an opportunity to reflect on this article of faith and to review the texts upon which it was based. As late as 1777, for example, Johnson resolved "to gather the arguments for Christianity" and in the last weeks of his life he discussed with William Windham his argument for belief in revelation.[20] It was the importance of these topics that brought Johnson back to the New Testament again and again and caused him to tell Mrs. Knowles that it was "the most difficult book in the world" to understand, the study of which required a lifetime.[21]

Almost as important as the Bible to Johnson was the *Book of Common Prayer*. In some way, in fact, it was more important because it administered more directly to Johnson's immediate spiritual needs. Whereas the Bible and especially the New Testament provided the ultimate religious basis for the Christian faith, the *Book of Common Prayer* sought to help man lead a better life through the confession of sins and the promise of repentance. Johnson knew virtually the entire work by heart, having started to memorize some of the passages at age four and having learned the rest through repeated use. He quoted from it freely, paraphrased it often, and made use of it in one way or another almost daily. Because he considered it central to the religious life of the practicing Christian, he "thought on writing a small book to teach the use of the Common Prayer" in 1766.[22] Johnson never wrote such a book, but on the basis of what we know about his own use it is easy to imagine what he might have said.

Its principal purpose would have been to provide the individual with an established order of worship by which he would acknowledge God's greatness, attest to his own sinfulness, seek repentance, and resolve to amend his life. It would have tried to set forth a pattern of religious devotion through the observance of which man could regain divine grace. This would have been its formal function, but it also would have sought to provide informal benefits. It would have aimed to act as an appropriate form of inspiration—and indeed of solace—when the individual was not in church but when he felt moved to confess his misguided ways and to seek new spiritual direction. That Johnson would have explored both approaches seems almost certain given his own habits. When he went to church he solemnly intoned the sanctioned prayers, but when he did not go, as for example on his birthday in 1764, he adapted the collect for that day and included it as part of his own prayer. "Last year," he noted, "I prayed on my birthday by accommodating the Morning collect for Grace, putting *year* for *day*. This I did this day."[23] By such means Johnson was able to fulfill religious obligations as well as to satisfy spiritual needs.

Johnson, in addition to these two major subjects of study, read widely in at least three other major areas of Christian thought. First, he was well versed in the writings of the Church Fathers. From the sale catalog of his library we know that he owned works of Augustine, Chrysostom, Ambrose, Origen, Athanasius, Eusebius, Ephraem Syrus, Basil, Justin Martyr, Clement of Alexandria, and Tertullian.[24] Most of these he must have read at random in order to learn more about the development of the early church, and in particular about the doctrinal differences that evolved. But Johnson never formally or systematically studied this subject until the last months of his life, when he appears to have been reading William Cave's biographical and critical study of these early figures entitled *Apostolici, or.... Lives . . . of the Primitive Fathers*.[25] Using this work as his guide,

Johnson began to read— and in most cases reread—many of the authors Cave had listed, moving chronologically from the first to the fourth century, from Saint Clement to Augustine. He made notes and underlinings, intending no doubt to return to particular authors, works, or passages. The project itself is remarkable for the self-discipline it demonstrates as well as for the seriousness with which Johnson approached this subject. He clearly thought of such an undertaking as one more way in which he might make himself more acceptable to his God.

As Sir John Hawkins observed, though Johnson "was competently skilled in the writings of the fathers, yet he was more conversant with those of the great English churchmen, namely, Hooker, Usher, Mede, Hammond, Sanderson, Hall, and others of that class." Johnson's initial interest in these figures had been largely historical. As the first important spokesmen for English Protestantism in the generation after the Elizabethan Settlement, they had helped to establish the Anglican church as the national Church of England. They had laid the historical groundwork for Johnson's own faith. But as he came to know them better he developed other grounds for his admiration, not the least of which was, as Hawkins again noted, "their skill in the Scriptures and the holiness of their lives." Johnson regarded these writers as subtle explicators of the holy word, fine stylists, and sound moralists. And it was for this combination of virtues that Johnson made such extensive use of them in the *Dictionary*. Finally, Johnson was attracted to many of the Puritan divines because of their mutual concern with the question of immortality. Hawkins was most explicit on this point. "To divert himself from a train of thinking which often involved him in a labyrinth of doubts and difficulties touching a future state of existence . . . he betook himself to the reading of books of practical divinity, and, among the rest, the writings of Baxter, and others of the old puritan and nonconforming divines."[26] Always eager to discover new models of devotion, Johnson often turned back to these figures for enlightenment and inspiration.

The last major area in which Johnson did a lot of religious reading was in the writing of his own age. Here he read widely in all things that pertained in any way to religion: ethics, metaphysics, prayer, church history, doctinal disputes. His greatest interests continued to be in the arguments for Christianity and in the way to become a better Christian. He was thus most attracted to Samuel Clarke, whom he considered to be the most substantial religious thinker of his age, owing to his efforts to provide a rational basis for belief, and to William Law, whom he had found to be "quite an overmatch" for him as a moralist. There is no need to discuss here the specific appeal of these men to Johnson since I have done that elsewhere. But it is important to stress that Johnson's religious reading of his contemporaries, like that of the Church Fathers and the Puritan divines, was motivated by the desire to keep himself informed as well as by the hope to discipline himself better in order that he might become a better Christian.

9

Of all the devotional measures that Johnson undertook to increase his piety, none was more important to him than prayer. He thought of it "as a reposal of myself upon God and a resignation of all into his holy hand," and though he cautioned against reasoning "too philosophically on the nature of prayer," he never doubted its efficacy.[27] "In truth," Johnson told Boswell, "we have the consent of all nations for the efficacy of prayer, whether offered up by individuals, or by assemblies; and Revelation has told us, it will be effectual."[28] Johnson considered the act of prayer as the most profound means by which he could communicate with God and by which he could rededicate himself to the religious life.

The purpose of prayer as Johnson conceived of it was threefold. It was first and foremost, as his definition makes clear, an act of submission. The individual must humble himself before God and promise obedience to his laws. His principal concern must be how best to please God. Johnson himself described this state of mind best when he resolved in one of his journals "to excite in myself such a fervent desire of pleasing God as should suppress all other passions."[29] It was, second, an act of self-examination in which the individual must review his conduct against the standard established by Christ and the Church, expressing gratitude for those instances where he has kept to the true path and remorse for those instances where he has strayed. His aim is to ascertain the extent of his spiritual progress by comparing past resolves with present practices and by recording the state of his spiritual condition. In this respect the act of prayer assumed for Johnson the same function as that of keeping a diary, namely, to record the history of one's mind. And Hawkins made this connection explicit when he suggested that Johnson kept a journal in order "to review his progress in life and to estimate his improvement in religion."[30] Finally, the purpose of prayer was to express repentance for past sins and to initiate appropriate reformation, which in Johnson's case almost always consisted of a list of resolves, some of which were sacred and some of which were not, but all of which contributed to his effort to regain God's grace. The ultimate function of prayer was the vigorous recommitment of the imperfect Christian soul to seek the perfection of the Christian ideal.

This conception of the function of prayer was not original to Johnson; it derived, of course, from the *Book of Common Prayer*. This great prayerbook was the obvious model for both the form—and indeed Johnson's conception of the function—of Johnson's own prayers. "I know," he once remarked, "of no good prayers but those in the *Book of Common Prayer*."[31] But the form of his own prayers owes as much to the spiritual needs of his own nature as it does to the solacing substance and stately rhythms of the Anglican prayerbook.

In composing his prayers his most common practice was to begin by making use of the opening of one of the well-known prayers from the *Book of Common Prayer*, such as the General Thanksgiving, and then gradually to depart from the established text to speak of his own concerns in a language that is distictly personal but still rich with the resonant tones of the prayerbook. Such was his habit when he wrote "his first solemn prayer" on his birthday in 1738.[32] He began with the opening of the Prayer for all Conditions of Men—"O God the Creatour and preserver of all Mankind"—and then abruptly switched to the first two sentences of the General Thanksgiving, which he at first paraphrased quite closely—"Father of all mercies, I thine unworthy servant do give thee most humble thanks, for all thy goodness and lovingkindness to me. I bless thee for my Creation, Preservation and Redemption, for the Knowledge of thy Son Jesus Christ, for the means of Grace, and the Hope of Glory." But at this point he became much more free and more personal in his treatment of the original text, abandoning its specific phrasing but retaining its spirit of gratitude and its desire for continued guidance. "In the days of Childhood and Youth, in the midst of weakness, blindness, and danger, Thou hast protected me; amidst Afflictions of

Mind, Body, and Estate thou hast supported me; and amidst vanity and Wickedness thou hast spared me." And here until the end of the prayer Johnson speaks in the characteristically fervent voice of the penitent who wishes to do all that he can to work out his salvation. In so doing, he expressed what were to become the central themes of these spiritual diaries. "And O Lord, enable me by thy Grace to use all diligence in redeeming the time which I have spent in Sloth, Vanity, and wickedness; to make use of they Gifts to the honour of thy Name; to lead a new life in thy Faith, Fear, and Love; and finally to obtain everlasting Life." And then, as if to complete the circle and to acknowledge his true source, Johnson closed the prayer with a variation upon the conclusion of the General Thanksgiving.

What Johnson had unconsciously evolved, and what he continued to use for the rest of his life, was a hybrid form, a cross between a standard prayer sanctioned by the Church and an entry in a private journal. And its great appeal for Johnson was that it derived formally from the liturgy of the Church but it provided him with great freedom of expression and great opportunity for religious intimacy. It satisfied his need for a formal act of prayer, for "a petition to heaven" as he defined it in the *Dictionary*, for formal communion with God. It also fulfilled his need for meditation, for "deep thought . . . thought employed upon sacred objects or occurrences, "as he stated in the *Dictionary*, for reflection upon his own spiritual condition. As eager as Johnson was to have an informal and confessional mode by which to express his religious feelings, nevertheless he was most reluctant to depart from the liturgical forms sanctioned by the Church. Fearful that he had indulged in excessive "longings of affection" for Tetty after her death, Johnson resolved: "I will however not deviate too much from common & received methods of devotion."[33] And thus the form of these spiritual reflections derived in part from the traditional prayers of the Church and in part from the needs of Johnson's own complex nature.

A careful reading of these important writings will reveal that they served two important functions for Johnson. First, they enabled him to keep a record of his spiritual progress. As he noted in a characteristic list of resolutions in 1755, his aim was "to examine the tenour of my life & particularly the last week & to mark my advances in religion or recession from it."[34] His aim was to record, and compare, and judge; it was to set down what he had done, to compare it with what he had intended to do; and then to make a moral judgement concerning his conduct. He most often engaged in this act of self-examination during Easter week or upon his birthday, when he seemed to be more than unusually conscious of the passage of time. Here is an excerpt from his birthday meditation of 1769:

> This day completes the sixtieth year of my age. What I have done and what I have left undone the unsettled state of my mind makes all endeavours to think improper. I hope to survey my life with more tranquility, in some part of the time which God shall grant me. . . . Almighty and most merciful Father, I now appear in thy presence laden with the sins, and accountable for the mercies of another year. Glory be to thee O God, for the mitigation of my troubles, and for the hope of health both of mind and body which thou hast vouchsafed me. Most merciful Lord . . . compose my mind, and relieve my diseases, enable me to perform the duties of my station . . . as that, when my hour of departure from this painful life shall be delayed no longer, I may be received to everlasting happiness.[35]

Such reviews were always painful to Johnson for the disparity they revealed between intention and performance. But he never abandoned them because he regarded them as an indispensable part of his quest for salvation.

The second important function that these writings served was to remind Johnson of the particular failings that impeded his spiritual progress as well as to incite in him new desire to amend his life. He knew that the worst of these failings was indolence, which he regarded as his "reigning sin" and which he felt was largely responsible for his other imperfections—his lack of religious discipline and his tendency to waste time. To impress upon himself the hold that such indolence had upon him and the destructive effect it had upon his efforts to attend church, read the Bible, and lead a more godly life, Johnson needed to record as often as he could the details of his religious life in order that he might initiate a proper course of repentance and reformation.

He defined repentance in the *Dictionary* as "sorrow for sin, such as produces newness of life," and he then quoted a pertinent passage from Henry Hammond that reflects Johnson's own view of the matter. "Repentance is a change of mind, or a conversion from sin to God; not some one bare act of change, but a lasting durable state of new life, which called regeneration." Johnson believed that it was not enough for man to feel sorrow for such sin; for repentance to be genuine it must result in discernible reformation. In one of the two sermons that Johnson wrote on the subject, he argued that "reformation is the chief part of repentance; not he that only bewails and confesses, but he that forsakes his sins, repents acceptably to God, that God who 'will have mercy and not sacrifice'; who will only accept a pure heart and real virtue, not outward forms of grief, or pompous solemnities of devotion" (Sermon 2).[36] Johnson considered all outward forms of repentance, such as tears and fainting, as affectation, as an attempt to express what custom demands rather than what the heart feels. Such manifestations of grief are useless because they do not contribute to the act of reformation or to the healthy resumption of life.

It was on these grounds that Johnson attacked the notion of retirement as an act of atonement because "any retirement from the world does not necessarily precede or follow repentance" (Sermon 2). Retirement from the world at various intervals to contemplate one's religious condition was useful because it helped to remind man of his true state and his true obligations. But there was no guarantee that such retirement could render repentance more sincere and reformation more probable. As he remarked to a nun in France, "Madam, you are here, not for the love of virtue, but the fear of vice."[37]

True reformation, as Johnson understood it, consisted of "not only the forbearance of those crimes of which we have been guilty, and the practice of those duties which we have hitherto neglected, but a reparation, as far as we are able to make it, of all the injuries that we have done, either to mankind in general, or to particular persons" (Sermon 2). Such reformation, furthermore, was always possible because God was merciful and because man had the necessary strength to amend his life if he so chose.

Johnson, however, was often less concerned about man's desire to seek repentance and reformation than he was about the various ways in which he rationalized the postponement of these measures. He never doubted man's theoretical commitment to these vital processes, but he did distrust, on the grounds of his own experience, man's practical conduct. This was his subject in

Sermon 10 where he argued that well-intentioned believers deferred the opportunity for regeneration by forgetting the demands of the religious life, by "setting the hour of death, and the day of account, at a great distance," and by assuming that there was plenty of time in which to repent. Such was not the case; for as Johnson observed, "we are in full possession of the *present* moment; let the *present* moment be improved; let that, which must necessarily be done sometime, be no longer neglected" (Sermon 10).

The illusion that there was ample time in which to repent, that life was long and death a remote prospect, was one major obstacle to early repentance. The other obstacle was habit. To have sinned once without punishment made it possible to sin again, and if this offense were not checked, it would become increasingly more difficult to resist. "But the time not only grows every day shorter, but the work to be performed in it more difficult; every hour, in which repentance is delayed, produces something new to be repented of. Habits grow stronger by long continuance, and passions more violent by indulgence" (Sermon 2). And to Johnson habit posed a much greater threat to any attempt at reformation than any other force because it operated in such a subtle way. An apparently trivial act, such as the failure to rise early on a regular basis, could gradually turn into a terrible case of indolence in which all activity bacame difficult. Physical indolence often led to psychological malaise. And so every effort had to be made to resist such weakness at its initial appearance—and at every subsequent reappearance—in order to prevent it gaining a more substantial hold. The only effective way to guard against submission to these seductive appeals was, as Johnson remarked, "to repair their negligence by vigilance and ardour" (Sermon 2).

Thus one of the main purposes of his prayers and meditations was to initiate a proper course of repentance and reformation by confessing his sins, by seeking forgiveness, by forswearing his foolish ways, and by forming new resolutions. Only in this way could he achieve proper religious devotion; only in this way could he purify his heart, discipline his mind, reclaim his imagination, and regulate his passions.

10

Boswell argued toward the end of the *Life* that Johnson's "Prayers and Meditations" demonstrated "beyond all his compositions for the publick, and all the eulogies of his friends and admirers, the sincere virtue and piety of Johnson. It proves with unquestionable authenticity, that amidst all his constitutional infirmities, his earnestness to conform his practice to the precepts of Christianity was unceasing, and that he habitually endeavoured to refer every transaction of his life to the will of the Supreme Being."[38] It is impossible to refute Boswell's claim; for there is no doubt about the sincerity with which Johnson approached his religious devotions and no doubt about his habitual effort to make his faith the center of his life. But it must be stressed as well that Johnson's devotional efforts were in themselves a cause of anxiety. He advised Boswell in composing his prayers "never lie in your prayers; never confess more than you really believe; never promise more than you mean to perform."[39] But he found it difficult to follow this advice. Fearful lest he fall prey to spiritual pride, Johnson often accused himself of sins that he had not committed. Determined to achieve greater religious self-mastery, Johnson often set himself tasks that he could not perform. And the inevitable result was that Johnson found himself caught in a vicious circle of guilt.

Distressed by his failure to conduct his life in accord with Christian principles, he had turned to the various measures described above in the hope that he might attain his goal, only to discover that he could not achieve such discipline and thus to experience further guilt and suffering. With each new attempt to amend his life, Johnson found it increasingly difficult to believe that he could ever achieve the reformation—and the peace of mind—he sought. And he would cry out: "Do I dare to resolve again?" Each time the answer was the same: "Yes, because reformation is necessary and despair is criminal." Johnson would not abandon the struggle; he would continue his spiritual pilgrimage. But the doubts and fears that had originally impelled him to undertake such devotional measures remained to haunt him, to drive him to seek yet greater piety, and, above all, to shape his character.

4

The Character of Fearing

When we came at the Hill Difficulty, he made no stick at that, nor did he much fear the Lyons. For you must know that his Trouble was not about such things as those, his Fear was about his Acceptance at last.

John Bunyan, *Pilgrim's Progress*

Your character is developed according to your faith. This is the primary religious truth from which no one can escape. Religion is the force of belief cleansing the inward parts.

Alfred North Whitehead,
Religion in the Making

Johnson's character is a superb example of the truth of Whitehead's assertion, as Johnson himself would have been the first to admit. He recognized that his mother's early religious instruction, his own spiritual struggles during adolescence, and his encounter with *A Serious Call* at Oxford had done much to determine his outlook. And he did not reject or regret this influence. On the contrary, he welcomed it in the belief that it had laid the foundation for his own character and conduct. As Boswell once remarked, "his piety being constant [was] the ruling principle of all his conduct."[1] Exposure to this Christian view of life had rescued him from one devastating depression and had helped him to redirect his life in a substantial way. And as a result Johnson had little sympathy with anyone who changed or abandoned his faith, as he made clear to his friend Mrs. Knowles, who defended the decision of a mutual acquaintance to leave the Church of England to become a Quaker.

> Johnson, (frowning very angrily,) 'Madam, she is an odious wench. She could not have any proper conviction that it was her duty to change her religion, which is the most important of all subjects, and should be studied with all care, and with all the helps we can get. She knew no more of the Church which she left, and that which she embraced, than she did of the difference between the Copernican and Ptolemaick systems.' Mrs. Knowles. 'She had the New Testament before her.' Johnson. 'Madam, she could not understand the New Testament, the most difficult book in the world, for which the study of a life is required.' Mrs. Knowles. 'It is clear as to essentials.' Johnson. 'But not as to controversial points. The heathens were easily converted, because they had nothing to give up; but we ought not, without very strong conviction indeed, to desert the religion in which we have been educated. That is the religion given you, the religion in which it may be said Providence has placed you. If you live conscientiously in that religion, you may be safe.'[2]

Johnson's passionate attack upon this innocent woman shocked those present; but it should not surprise us, especially when we regard it as a measure of Johnson's deep belief in the power of religious faith to mold character and determine conduct. Implicit in this outburst was Johnson's fear that to change one's faith was to risk the loss of a coherent sense of self and of a meaningful view of life. And that was to be avoided at all costs.

Johnson's own faith, as we have just seen, was a much more complex and troubled matter for him than it at first appeared. He was torn between his desire to make his faith the center of his life and his fear that he could not do so. He sought to establish a rational basis for his faith only to discover that such certitude could not be provided—at least to his satisfaction. He struggled to lead a virtuous life in strict accord with Christian principles only to be haunted by his own failures and his own unworthiness. His religious belief, in short, had developed in part as a result of his early training but in greater part as a reaction to certain needs, to certain doubts and fears, that had to be met or managed in order for Johnson to function as a productive human being. And his religious life can be best understood as a lifelong attempt to come to terms with these psychological forces.

In a famous passage in the *Life,* Boswell described in a memorable metaphor the terrible conflict Johnson had with his fears as well as the heroic way in which he tried to overcome them. "His mind resembled the vast amphitheatre, the Colisaeum at Rome. In the centre stood his judgement, which, like a mighty gladiator, combated those apprehensions that, like the wild beasts of the *Arena,* were all around in cells, ready to be let out upon him. After a conflict, he drove them back into their dens; but not killing them, they were still assailing him."[3]

The brilliance of this passage lies in Boswell's portrait of Johnson as a mighty gladiator, fighting in the vast arena of his soul the frightful demons of doubt and fear. The particular apprehension Boswell had in mind was that of death, but as his inspired metaphor makes clear, he was well aware that Johnson wrestled with other dark, hostile forces. What Boswell glimpsed but did not fully grasp was that Johnson's character had developed in response to certain religious fears that were deeply rooted in his nature and that, if he had been unable to control them, would have plunged him into despair. Thus the central elements of his complex character—his love of life, his cultivation of reason, his inquiry into the workings of the mind, and his moral seriousness—all evolved as a defense against despair, as attempts to manage himself and regulate his life so that he could work out his salvation.

2

The first and most famous of these fears was that of death. As he himself admitted, "he never had a moment in which death was not terrible to him," and he felt that "the whole of life [was] but keeping away the thoughts of it."[4] As terrible as this fear was to Johnson, he nevertheless believed that it was present in all men to some degree and that there was no perfect way by which we could "fortify our minds for the approach of death." He was thus especially impatient with anyone who said he was willing to die or who claimed he felt no such fear. When Boswell, for example, told Johnson that Dr. Dodd had said that he was willing to die, Johnson did not believe him. "Dr. Dodd," he pointedly replied, "would have given both his hands and both his legs to have lived."[5] And he was even more scornful of David Hume, whom Boswell had reported had died without fear and with perfect peace of mind. Johnson thought such conduct was in some ways to be expected from a man who had not read the New Testament "with attention" and who had been "at no pains to inquire into the truth of religion," but he asserted finally that such conduct could only be explained as a desire "to assume an appearance of ease."[6] It was not genuine; it was pure affectation.

Although Johnson believed that "hardly any man died without affectation," he was still disdainful of those who tried to conceal their fear behind a mask of serenity.[7] He even reprimanded Mrs. Thrale on this point. "Write to me no more about *dying with a grace.* When you feel what I have felt in approaching Eternity—in fear of soon hearing the sentence of which there is no revocation, you will know the folly."[8] Thus as horrific as the thought of death was to Johnson and as often as he cut Boswell short on this subject, he still believed, as Jean Hagstrum has convincingly argued, that it was the inescapable fact of death that gave life much of its meaning. Johnson knew that without a profound apprehension of death man would not be impelled to work out his salvation.[9]

The ultimate origin of Johnson's fear of death was, as Boswell first pointed out, "the result of philosophic and religious consideration."[10] Part of this fear sprang from philosophic reflection upon death as the end of life and as the extinction of our earthly selves. As such, it was a fear that arose from Johnson's acute sense of the finitude of life, of how little time each of us has in which to work out our salvation. This was one of the great themes of Johnson's writing and nowhere did it receive more poignant expression than at the end of *Idler* 103. "This secret horror of the last," as he called it, "is inseparable from a thinking being whose life is limited, and to whom death is dreadful. We always make a secret comparison between a part and the whole; the termination of any period of life reminds us that life itself has likewise its termination; when we have done anything for the last time, we involuntarily reflect that a part of the days allotted us is past, and that as more is past there is less remaining."

But by far the greatest part of this fear arose from Johnson's religious conviction, first acquired from his mother, that the fact of death was inseparable from the act of divine judgment. At the hour of his own death, he believed that he would be either damned or saved, and since he did not hold that this issue could be known or resolved in advance, he existed in agonizing uncertainty. "Some people," he conceded, "are not afraid, because they look upon salvation as the effect of an absolute decree, and think they feel in themselves the marks of sanctification." However, "others," as Johnson insisted, clearly thinking of himself, "and those the most rational in my opinion, look upon salvation as conditional; and as they never can be sure that they have complied with the conditions, they are afraid."[11]

Although Johnson's mother had some Calvinist strains in her faith and may have unconsciously given some credence to them in her instruction of her son, nevertheless the mature Johnson never subscribed to the doctrine of predestination and never permitted anyone to defend philosophical determinism. He was always a vigorous champion of free will, even if he sometimes seemed to protest too much. He believed that man, in spite of his innate sinfulness, could regain divine grace and achieve salvation. But man could never be certain in this life about his ultimate destiny. "He owned," as Boswell recorded in a poignant passage, "that our being in an unhappy uncertainty as to our salvation was mysterious; and said, "Ah! we must wait till we are in another state of being, to have many things explained to us."[12] And just as he was impatient with anyone who denied having a fear of death, so did he refuse to think better of a man "who should tell me on his death-bed he was sure of salvation. A man cannot be sure himself that he has divine intimation of acceptance; much less can he make others sure that he has it."[13] Johnson was never sure himself and as a result dreaded that moment when he would die and when he would be judged.

3

Johnson's principal reaction to this fear of death was to immerse himself in life. He sought to lose himself in all that life had to offer and to steep himself in its infinite novelty and tantalizing variety. It is this quality that Joseph Wood Krutch had in mind when he wrote of Johnson's "zest for living." Part of this zest was instinctive: it was a love of life that Johnson had possessed from the start. Like Thoreau when he went to Walden, Johnson throughout his life "wished to live deliberately, to front only the essential facts of life, and see if [he] could not learn what it had to teach, and not, when [he] came to die, discover that [he] had not lived."[14] But most of this zest was acquired: it sprang from his fear of death and annihilation. "Death had always been to him an object of terrour; so that, though by no means happy, he still clung to life with an eagerness at which many have wondered. At any time when he was ill, he was very much pleased to be told that he looked better."[15]

Johnson recognized from the outset that he could not "think down" such a fear any more than he could "wrestle down" his melancholy. "To attempt to *think them down,*" he told Boswell, "is madness."[16] He realized that man had no choice but to seek to divert his mind from such troubling thoughts by fixing it on other objects and by immersing himself in the present. What Johnson wrote in *Rambler* 89 about how best to recover one's freedom from the tyranny of the imagination can be equally well applied to the principal means by which he sought to dispel his fears of death. "In order to regain liberty, [a man] must find the means of flying from himself; he must, in opposition to the Stoick precept, teach his desires to fix upon external things; he must adopt the joys and pains of others, and excite in his mind the want of social pleasures and amicable communication." And it was this prescription that Johnson sought to apply to himself.

Johnson thus anticipated, as W. Jackson Bate pointed out over twenty years ago, Freud's theory of repression, the process by which man attempts to dispel his fears by fixing his mind on new concerns.[17] The forces that Freud had in mind were, of course, mainly sexual whereas those that concerned Johnson were what we would now call existential. They pertained to the problems that man encountered as he tried to grasp the meaning of life. By recognizing the existence of such fears in the human psyche and by analyzing how such forces shaped human character and destiny, Johnson anticipated not only Freud but also Kierkegaard.

Long before Kierkegaard wrote, Johnson had started to explore the way in which human character developed as a response to the uncertainties and perplexities of existence. And he stressed, furthermore, as Kierkegaard later would, that man's deepest need was to learn how to live with a sense of anxiety, with what Johnson on one occasion called "the pain of being a man."* Johnson would have agreed with Kierkegaard's assertion that "there lives not one single man who after all is not to some extent in despair, in whose inmost parts there does not dwell a disquietude, a perturbation, a discord, an anxious dread of an unknown something, or of a something he does not even dare to make acquaintance with, dread of a possibility of life, or dread of himself. . . . At any rate there has lived no one and there lives no one outside of Christendom who is not in despair."[18] And he also would have agreed that the only possible way to counteract this powerful force was to acquire what Kierkegaard called "a theological self," a self that could stand "directly in the sight of God," and that evolved not so much from doing good as by having faith. As Johnson himself remarked in Sermon 10, "to live religiously, is to walk, not by sight, but by faith; to act in confidence of things unseen, in hope of future recompense, and in fear of future punishment." Faith for him, as indeed for Kierkegaard, was the "firm belief that whatever evils are suffered to befall [man] will finally contribute to his felicity" (Sermon 14). But Johnson found it extremely difficult to develop this theological self and evolved instead as his defense against his fear of death an intense involvement in life itself. His response to the horrors of death—and indeed to the anxieties created by life itself—was to immerse himself in this life and to trust in God.

4

The most immediate effect that Johnson's immersion in life had upon the formation of his character was to create in him a passionate love of activity as an end in itself. Commenting in *Rambler* 25 on its inherent therapeutic value, Johnson observed

---

*Johnson himself often used the word *anxiety* in this way in his own writings. And he defined it in the *Dictionary* as "trouble of mind, about some future event; suspense with uneasiness; perplexity; solicitude." He quoted here a passage from John Tillotson to illustrate his definition: "To be happy, is not only to be freed from the pains and diseases of the body but from anxiety and vexation of spirit, not only to enjoy the pleasures of sense, but peace of conscience and tranquility of mind."

that "activity" carries within itself the seeds of its own "reformation." He believed that the process by which man becomes involved in anything, especially when he is feeling indolent or depressed, could not help but rescue him from a precipitous descent into psychological paralysis. Activity, or what he often called employment, bred health through involvement while indolence encouraged disease through stasis and passivity. It was this conviction that inspired him to alter the conclusion of Robert Burton's *Anatomy of Melancholy* from "be not solitary, be not idle" to "if you are idle, be not solitary; if you are solitary, be not idle."[19] To create and sustain emotional health man must have the willingness and the courage to become involved in large and important ways. He must shun solitude and resist indolence; he must seek out society and embrace life. And this Johnson did to such a remarkable degree that it became one of the salient features of his character.

His love of activity manifested itself in three significant ways. The first was psychological. Although no man was more impatient than Johnson with what he called "bustle," which he once described as "getting on horseback in a ship," nevertheless few men knew better than Johnson what a fine line there was between those pursuits that were truly senseless and those that genuinely diverted the mind from darker thoughts.[20] He also knew better than most men how important such apparently meaningless pursuits could be both to deal with the demands of daily life and to insure sustained mental health. "The art is," as he observed in *Idler* 31, "to fill the day with petty business, to have always something in hand which may raise curiosity, but not solicitude, and keep the mind in a state of action, but not of labour." Such an art involved a delicate balance but one that was vital to human happiness.

The second manifestation of this activity was intellectual. It revealed itself in the numerous intellectual projects that Johnson undertook throughout his life, from the abortive proposal to edit Angelus Politian to the magisterial production of the *Dictionary*. Most of these projects, of course, related directly to his professional life, to his need to support himself, to his desire for recognition of his abilities, and to his thirst for fame. Many more of them, however, evolved from Johnson's extraordinary intellectual curiosity to know as much as he could about the world in which he lived. These pursuits ranged from his study of the

Greek classics at Oxford, to his lifelong interest in religion and philosophy, to his prayers upon "the study of tongues" and "before the study of law," to his so-called reportium, his list of reading and notes that he drew up just six weeks before he died. And this list of subjects does not begin to touch upon those that always interested him but that he never studied seriously, such as economics, trade, politics, and what we would now call sociology. His aim in all of these intellectual endeavors was as much to promote knowledge and secure his own well being as it was to divert his mind from more disturbing thoughts.

And finally, much of Johnson's activity was physical. The long walks to Birmingham and back that he made in 1729 as well as his later love of exercise—of horseback riding, of swimming, and above all of walking—were examples of the extent to which he valued bodily exercise as a source of health and sanity. Related to this kind of activity was his love of travel. Although hindered in the first half of his life from travel by his impoverished circumstances, once he had received his pension he not only went to Scotland, Wales, and France but also traveled a great deal within England. He returned often to Oxford and Lichfield; he accompanied Sir Joshua Reynolds to Devonshire; and he journeyed often to Brighton with the Thrales. Part of this passion was intellectual: he wanted to see how others lived and to compare their customs with his own. But part of it was psychological: he wanted new things to fill up his mind and he wanted to experience new sensations. He never saw the Great Wall in China or the great civilizations of the Mediterranean as he had hoped, but that he saw as much as he did was a testament both to his intellectual energy and to his belief in the healing power of activity itself.

5

The second important way in which Johnson immersed himself in human life was to "adopt the joys and pains of others." Eager to escape from his own fears and naturally sympathetic with the plight of others, Johnson developed an extraordinary compassion for his fellow man. It most often expressed itself as an intense concern for anyone who had experienced the essential misery of life. He was especially sympathetic with anyone who was poor, or who had experienced a sudden calamity, or who had suffered the death of a friend. "And here," noted Sir John Hawkins, "I cannot forbear remarking, that, almost throughout his life, poverty and distressed circumstances seemed to be the strongest of all recommendations to his favour."[21] Never forgetting his own struggle against poverty and those long years of obscurity, Johnson took every opportunity he got to help those who were in any kind of distress. As Mrs. Thrale observed, "he loved the lower ranks of humanity with a real affection: and though his talents and learning kept him always in the sphere of upper life, yet he never lost sight of the time when he and they shared pain and pleasure in common."[22]

This compassion for others was in itself responsible for two other important qualities of Johnson's character. The first was charity. Johnson had a firm belief in the importance of performing some kind act each day. A friend once observed Johnson "tugging at a nail which he was endeavouring to extract from the bark of a plum tree; and having accomplished it, he exclaimed, 'There, Sir, I have done *some* good today; the tree might have festered. I make a rule, Sir, to do some good every day of my life.'"[23] Such was his conception of charity, of which the most obvious manifestation was his celebrated love—and treatment—of the poor. "He loved the poor," as Mrs. Thrale remarked, "as I never yet saw any one else do, with an earnest desire to make them happy."[24] And she was right. He treated them as equals, gave them money, offered them shelter, and lodged many of them in his own house. He himself lived on scarcely seventy pounds a year and gave away all the rest. Mrs. Thrale was also quite sure that he had given "away all he had, and all he had ever gotten, except the two thousand pounds he left behind; and the very small portion of his income which he spent on himself."[25] And he always gave without expectation of services in return and without moralism. When asked by a friend about a poor woman to whom he had given a half-crown but who appeared the following day in church "in long sleeves and ribands," Johnson replied, "and if it gave the woman pleasure, why should she not wear them?"[26] He gave freely and generously because he believed if he "did not assist them no one else would, and they must be lost for want."[27] It was this conviction that impelled him to carry home a down-and-out prostitute as well as to stuff pennies into the hands of children who lay asleep in their mothers' arms in the streets.

Johnson's charity did not confine itself exclusively to the

anonymous poor; it was extended as well to many of his friends who found themselves in any form of distress. Many of these actions also assumed a monetary form, but just as often they involved some thoughtful contribution to the solution of a literary or intellectual problem. Sometimes the effort was relatively minor, as when he helped Goldsmith revise the final lines of *The Deserted Village* or when he advised Boswell on certain complex points of Scottish law. On other occasions, his assistance was much more substantial, as when he prompted Robert Chambers in the composition of the Vinerian law lectures. Finally, the most poignant manifestation of Johnson's charity was the concern that he demonstrated for those who had experienced psychological collapse. His sympathy for William Collins and his visits to Christopher Smart in Bedlam both attest to the real tenderness of heart that he felt for those afflicted with the loss of their reason. That he would not turn his back on them and that he would help them in any way he could is one of the most striking instances of his genuine concern for the plight of others. As Goldsmith himself said of Johnson, "no man alive [had] a more tender heart."[28]

The other important by-product of his compassion was his great capacity for friendship. From his earliest years in Lichfield to his last days in London, Johnson was always trying to make new friendships and to maintain old ones. Some of this desire sprang from his instinctive love of people, but most of it derived from his fear of loneliness and his horror of self-confrontation. "If a man does not make new acquaintance as he advances through life, he will soon find himself left alone. A man, Sir, should keep his friendship *in constant repair.*"[29] Such was his justification for the formation of new friendships, but he felt just as strongly about the maintenance of old ties. "To let friendship die away by negligence and silence," he wrote to Bennet Langton in 1782, "is certainly not wise. It is voluntarily to throw away one of the greatest comforts of this weary pilgrimage, of which when it is, as it must be, taken finally away, he that travels on alone, will wonder how his esteem could be so little."[30]

Johnson needed friends to help him fill up the day and to comfort him in times of distress. His new friends were almost always younger and were people Johnson met after he came up to London in 1737. Some of them, like Richard Savage and Edward Cave, were men he came to know through his literary pursuits;

and some of them, like the Thrales and Boswell, were people he met after he had acquired his reputation as the leading man of letters of his age. In all cases, what was remarkable about Johnson's friends was that they came from all walks of life, were of all ages and dispositions, and were always treated by him with affection and respect. But Johnson tended to reserve his deepest affection for his old friends, for men like Edmund Hector and John Taylor, whom he had known since childhood in Lichfield. We sense much of this deep feeling in a letter he wrote Boswell upon discovering on a visit to Lichfield in 1777 that his old friend, Harry Jackson, had died. "It was a loss, and a loss not to be repaired, as he was one of the companions of my childhood. I hope we may long continue to gain friends, but the friends which merit or usefulness can procure us, are not able to supply the place of old acquaintance, with whom the days of youth may be retraced, and those images revived which gave the earliest delight."[31] And it was in particular to Hector and Taylor that Johnson turned late in his life to find the companionship that he had lost with the death of Henry Thrale and the remarriage of Mrs. Thrale. Writing to Hector in the late 1770s Johnson observed, "you and I should now naturally cling to one another: we have outlived most of those who could pretend to rival us in each other's kindness. In our walk through life we have dropped our companions, and are now to pick up such as chance may offer us, or travel on alone. You, indeed, have a sister, with whom you can divide the day: I have no natural friend left; but Providence has been pleased to preserve me from neglect; I have not wanted such alleviations of life as friendship could supply."[32] Friendship for Johnson, at the end of his life as at the beginning, was one of the principal means by which he endured life. In being able to enter into the lives of others, and in being able to share their hopes and fears, Johnson was able to forget for a while his own anxieties.

6

The third major consequence of Johnson's desire to immerse himself in life was to create in him a passionate love of diversion, which he defined in the *Dictionary* as "sport, something that unbends the mind by turning it off from care." As he himself admitted and as his friends repeatedly testified, Johnson welcomed any opportunity to take his mind off his own cares any way he could. And his most favorite form of diversion was good talk.

Johnson is, of course, famous for his talk. He was widely admired for it by his contemporaries while alive and upon his death has passed into legend as one of the great talkers of all time. Almost everyone can quote something from Johnson and almost everyone has assumed that this gift was innate, that he was born speaking in the aphoristic and authoritative style that is linked to his name. What few have realized is that Johnson decided at an early age that conversation was an important part of human experience and that he should become as proficient in it as he could. When asked by Sir Joshua Reynolds how he acquired his extraordinary fluency of speech, he replied that "he had early laid it down as a fixed rule to do his best on every occasion, and in every company; to impart whatever he knew in the most forcible language he could put it in; and that by constant practice, and never suffering any careless expressions to escape him . . . it became habitual to him.[33]

Johnson prized good talk, as he most often called it, in part because, as Boswell observed, he considered "conversation as a trial of intellectual vigor and skill." Johnson loved to exercise his mind just as a fine athlete likes to test his body, namely, for the sheer delight of feeling it work. He hoped, of course, that the products of his thought would be of use to his listener, but he did not believe that good talk would ever be a true substitute for reading or serious, systematic study. "The foundation [for knowledge]," he made clear to Boswell, "must be laid by reading. General principles must be had from books, which, however, must be brought to the test of real life. In conversation you never get a system. What is said upon a subject is to be gathered from a hundred people. The parts of a truth, which a man gets thus, are at such a distance from each other, that he never attains to a full view."[34] It is this notion that was responsible for another reason why Johnson valued good talk. Contrary to the impression that Boswell sometimes gives of Johnson in the *Life,* Johnson loved conversation not so that he might disparage his listener but that he might increase social pleasure. He cherished bright, witty talk for the genuine pleasure it afforded, but was shrewd enough to realize that such moments occur only "where there is no competition, no vanity, but a calm quiet interchange of sentiments."[35] Despite his tendency "to talk for victory" and to beat his opponents down, Johnson felt that the most pleasant moments of social intercourse occurred where there was no such confrontation and where there was no desire to arrive at a conclusion. He disagreed with a friend who complained of poor conversation at dinner parties by arguing that the purpose of such gatherings was not good talk but "to eat and drink together, and to promote kindness; and, Sir, this is better done when there is no solid conversation; for when there is, people differ in opinion, and get into bad humour."[36] And he genuinely believed, as he himself said, that "the happiest conversation is that of which nothing is distinctly remembered but a general effect of pleasing impression."[37] Life on the whole presented very few such moments and they were thus to be enjoyed when they occurred.

But above all, Johnson longed for good conversation because it freed him from the horror of solitude and engaged his often vacant mind with appealing hopes. He depended on conversation, be it with good friends or total strangers, to get outside of his self-created prison, where he was so often enchained by his own irrational fears. What he said of Mr. Sober's love of conversation in *Idler* 31 could well be said of his own: "Mr. Sober's chief pleasure is conversation; there is no end of his talk or his attention; to speak or to hear is equally pleasing; for he still fancies that he is teaching or learning something, and is free for the time from his own reproaches." Good talk, like anything else that could rivet the attention of the mind, permitted the momentary joy of self-forgetfulness and rare relief from self-reproach.

There were inevitably, of course, those terrible moments when neither company nor conversation was available, when the taverns had closed and when friends had grown tired and gone home to bed. Johnson so dreaded these moments that he postponed them for as long as he could, often even accompanying his friends down "the first pair of stairs, in some hopes that they may, perhaps, return again."[38] He even induced Dr. Levet and Anna Williams to stay up until he came home so that he would not be alone. In short, he went to extraordinary lengths to avoid being alone, especially at night, when he was almost certain to be besieged by fears of inadequacy and guilt.

At such times, whether during the day or night, Johnson resorted to a variety of devices by which he distracted himself from excessive reflection upon his uncertain spiritual condition. Sometimes he could put his mind at rest by reading or writing.

But all too often he found reading dull and writing too much like work. At other times, when he felt a more urgent need to fix his mind on some specific object, he would engage like Sober in manual arts or perform chemical experiments in which he would count the drops of liquid as they fell from his vial and try to forget "that while a drop is falling, a moment flies away." At still other times, when his mind was very disturbed indeed, he would set himself some problem of arithmetic or engage in some bizarre act of measurement. He tried on one occasion to establish the rate at which his fingernails grew, and on another the speed with which hair grew on his chest, and on another to compare the weight of forty vine leaves before they dried and afterward. Such extreme measures are notable in themselves but assume even greater significance for the way in which they demonstrate how perilous Johnson's psychological balance was. And it was on such particularly dark occasions that Johnson most probably surrendered from time to time to drink.

From an account of his drinking that he gave to Boswell and that is recorded in the *Life*, it would appear that Johnson virtually abstained from drink from 1736 to 1757, after which he took it up with moderation, only to give it up eight years later owing to illness for the rest of his life.[39] But it is also clear, by Johnson's own admission, that in spite of a life spent in almost virtual abstinence from wine and spirits, there were significant exceptions. There was, for example, Reynolds' account of watching Johnson drink three bottles of port in one evening. But much more importantly, Johnson admitted that "I have drunk many a bottle by myself; in the first place, because I had need of it to raise my spirits; in the second place, because I would have nobody to witness its effects upon me."[40]

Johnson did not drink much in public because he could not do so in moderation and because he felt it improved neither the mind nor social intercourse. On the other hand, he openly admitted that he needed wine to endure those moments when self-reproach became severe. The following exchange between Johnson and John Spottiswoode, a Scottish solicitor, makes this need clear. "Johnson. 'I require wine, only when I am alone. I have then often wished for it, and often taken it.' Spottiswoode. 'What, by way of a companion, Sir? Johnson. 'To get rid of myself, to send myself away.'"[41] And Johnson made very much the same sort of reply when Mrs. Williams once wondered "what pleasure men can take in making beasts of themselves." Johnson pointedly responded, "I wonder, Madam, that you have not penetration enough to see the strong inducement to this excess; for he who makes a *beast* of himself gets rid of the pain of being a man."[42] It was the continual consciousness of this pain that was at the heart of Johnson's passionate search for diversion as well as of his passionate immersion in life itself.

7

Almost as profound as his fear of death was his fear of madness. "To Johnson," observed Boswell, "whose supreme enjoyment was the exercise of his reason, the disturbance or obscuration of that faculty was the evil most to be dreaded. Insantiy, therefore, was the object of his most dismal apprehension."[43] Unlike his attitude toward death, however, Johnson did not believe that this fear was inherent in all men, but he did think that more people suffered from some form of mental distress than many others suspected. Imlac made just this point to the travelers in *Rasselas* when they mocked the claims of the mad astronomer. "Disorders of intellect," he reminded them, "happen much more often than superficial observers will easily believe. Perhaps, if we speak with rigorous exactness, no human mind is in its right state. There is no man whose imagination does not sometimes predominate over his reason, who can regulate his attention wholly by his will, and whose ideas will come and go at his command. No man will be found in whose mind airy notions do not sometimes tyrannize, and force him to hope or fear beyond the limits of sober probability. All power of fancy over reason is a degree of insanity; but while this power is such as we can control and repress, it is not visible to others, nor considered as any depravation of the mental faculties: it is not pronounced madness but when it comes ungovernable, and apparently influences speech or action."[44] Besides making clear what a fine line Johnson thought there was between sanity and insanity, this passage also reveals a problem of definition. What did Johnson mean by madness?

In his conversation, as Boswell noted on one occasion, Johnson tended to confuse madness with melancholy and to use the two terms indiscriminately. He did not think of melancholy as either the cause or a less intense form of madness but linked the two together as a state of emotional and mental disorder. Only in *Rasselas*—and to a certain degree in the *Dictionary*—did he make clear that madness meant a state in which man's reason no longer functions properly. But nowhere did he distinguish this state from that of melancholy. We do best, therefore, to accept the distinction that Boswell made after having reflected on the problem himself and after having consulted a distinguished authority, Professor Gaubius of Leyden. "But there is surely a clear distinction between a disorder which affects only the imagination and spirits, while the judgement is sound, and a disorder by which the judgement itself is impaired."[45]

Johnson almost certainly would have accepted this distinction and might have admitted as well that he experienced a depression of spirits on numerous occasions but that only rarely had he feared for the loss of his reason. Such a moment most probably occurred in 1730 and then again in the 1760s, when he gave the celebrated padlock to Mrs. Thrale. There were undoubtedly other moments in which he lived on the edge of madness but from which he was rescued by a friend or some unexpected diversion. Madness, then, meant to Johnson "the uncertain continuance of reason" and was characterized by a complete loss of self-control. It was this state that Imlac described as "the most dreadful and alarming" of all our uncertainties.

The precise origin of Johnson's fear is difficult to locate since he almost never discussed the matter and since he did not permit Boswell to bring it up. He told Boswell on their tour through Scotland that he had inherited "a vile melancholy from [his] father which [had] made [him] mad all his life, at least not sober."[46] Although he undoubtedly knew that it was impossible to inherit such a condition, nevertheless his remark reflects his belief that this affliction was chronic, if not innate. On only one other occasion did he speculate about its cause, suggesting that it was "occasioned by too much indulgence of imagination." What he meant was that madness arose when reason was no longer able to control the fanciful promptings of the imagination. Reason was the principal means by which he sought self-understanding and self-control. To lose the use of this faculty was to abandon himself to the real but largely unidentified beasts of Boswell's symbolic arena. It meant to fall prey to excessive and irrational reflection upon the discrepancy that inevitably developed between hope and reality, between promise and performance. And it was his extraordinary sensitivity to this disparity that was the ultimate cause of his madness.

8

Johnson's reaction to his fear of insanity was to develop a passionate interest in how to govern the mind. This interest—and its intellectual and moral consequences—was so important to him that it became the second distinctive quality of his character. He was fascinated by how the mind worked in itself and, in particular, by the effect that the rational faculty had upon human conduct. He thought of the mind as a battlefield in which reason was always struggling against the imagination for control of the heart of man. And he believed furthermore that the few moments of human happiness that man could know depended entirely on man's ability to insure the triumph of reason over the self-deceptive forces of the imagination.

He gave as his first definition of reason in the *Dictionary* "the power by which man deduces one proposition from another, or proceeds from premises to consequences, the rational faculty." He then cited a passage from Hooker's *Laws of Ecclesiastical Polity* which Johnson uses to clarify his conception of the origin and nature of reason: "Reason is the director of man's will, discovering in action what is good; for the laws of well-doing are the dictates of right reason." Johnson accepted with complete confidence the traditional view of reason held by such Christian humanists as Hooker and Milton, who believed that reason was implanted in man by God to enable him to do good if he so desired. He further shared their conviction that although it was principally through reason that man acquired knowledge, nevertheless the highest use to which such knowledge should be put was moral. The real end of knowledge was to promote virtue. And in order to permit the possible realization of such virtue, it was imperative to protect the rational faculty from all forces that sought to undermine it. "He therefore that would govern his actions by the laws of virtue," Johnson observed in *Rambler* 8, "must regulate his thoughts by those of reason; he must keep guilt from the recesses of his heart, and remember that the pleasures of fancy, and the emotions of desire are more dangerous as they are more hidden, since they escape the awe of observation, and operate equally in every situation, without the concurrence of external opportunities."

Johnson was quick to admit that various external forces were of sufficient strength to paralyze or seriously impair the rational faculty. Of these, the most deceptive and seductive were "the pleasures of fancy" and "the emotions of desire." These were to be distrusted because, if pursued without appropriate awareness, they led to deep dissatisfaction and delusion. The great enemy of reason, and indeed of human happiness, was the imagination because it encouraged man to develop unrealistic expectations of himself and of life itself. It encouraged him to pursue desires that either could not be realized themselves or, if they were realized, created no lasting satisfaction. The pursuit of perfect knowledge was just as futile ultimately as that of fame. The scholar who took all knowledge as his province was destined to be just as disappointed and frustrated as the author in search of everlasting fame. No human desire could assure permanent satisfaction. The nature of such desire was to seek fulfillment, which, once realized, only created new desires. The cycle was endless and the disappointment inevitable. Just as serious, moreover, was the power of the imagination to deceive man into believing that he was a much more substantial figure than he truly was. The astronomer in *Rasselas* is a superb example of the terrible delusion that man can suffer when he lets his imagination be fed by his pride and so nourishes the notion that he can control the movements of the planets and the vagaries of the weather. When we first meet him he is in fact a madman who reminds us more of the scientists at Lagado in book 3 of *Gulliver's Travels* than he does of anyone else.

The imagination, in short, when it does get astride of man's reason, produces only intellectual and moral chaos. It prevents man from ordering his own nature sensibly as well as from seeing the possibilities of his life with a clear, dispassionate, and unillusioned eye. And it was the opportunity for self-understanding and self-control that led Johnson to value his rational faculty above all else.

Contrary to popular belief, Johnson was a psychologist first and a moralist second. His deepest desire was to understand how the mind worked and to analyze the various forces that determined human conduct. This effort of understanding always began at home; it always began with himself and his own experience. And yet it always aimed, even at the outset, beyond himself, at other people whom he did not know but who he was sure suffered from the same affliction that he did. This was the characteristic movement of his mind—from the particular to the general, from the psychological to the moral—and it was also the predominant rhetorical pattern of his periodical writing.

Most of these essays move from an opening section in which the subject is introduced, to a long middle part in which the origin, nature, and appeal of the problem are explored, to a short conclusion in which a remedy is offered. *Rambler* 134 is an especially fine example of the way in which Johnson's struggle for self-understanding led him to an awareness that transcended his own predicament and related to all men and women. It begins with Johnson's description of his inability to choose a topic for the essay due that day and being forced, by the arrival of the printer's boy, to write. We begin with a real problem that Johnson faced, and yet very rapidly we are forced to see his particular dilemma as part of a larger human failing, "the folly of allowing ourselves to delay what we know cannot be finally escaped." At this point, Johnson begins what is always the most arresting and substantial part of the essay, namely, his analysis of the psychological appeal of forces that attract us but that we know are of no use to us. Habitually sympathetic to human weakness, Johnson sets forth clearly but gently the psychological appeal of inactivity as well as some of its specific causes. And then, in the last paragraph, having shown how foolish it is to defer any meaningful pursuit, he forces his reader to consider the true folly of such behavior given "the certainty that life cannot be long, and the probability that it will be much shorter than nature allows." In a closing sentence, reminiscent of Sir Thomas Browne, Johnson raises his argument to a moral plane toward which he has been pointing from the start. "It is true that no diligence can ascertain success; death may intercept the swiftest career; but he who is cut off in the execution of an honest undertaking, has at least the honour of falling in his rank, and has fought the battle, though he missed the victory."

What should now be clear is that the most profound effect that Johnson's fear of insanity had upon his character was to create in him a lifelong fascination with the drama enacted in the human mind. He wanted to understand as best he could the conscious and unconscious forces that determined human conduct. He wanted to see them for what they were so that when he encountered them he could recognize them and know best how to overcome them. And he regarded such knowledge as the most important that he or any man could possess, not only for the self-mastery that it permitted but also for the indispensible assistance it provided in his quest for redemption. If he were not in control of his faculties, how could he ever hope to work out his salvation?

9

The third great fear that haunted Johnson was that he had misspent his life. He feared that he had become too involved in the mundane matters of the present and had thus ignored the more lasting concerns of the future. He believed, as Law had exhorted in *A Serious Call*, that "the right religious use of every thing and every talent, is the indispensable duty of every being that is capable of knowing right and wrong,"[47] but he found it difficult to practice this precept from day to day. He was torn between how he could retain his sense of personal identity and still remain a servant of God; he was torn between his desire to enjoy this life and yet prepare himself properly for the life to come. The question he faced, as Ernest Becker has phrased it, is: "how does one lean on God and give over everything to Him and still stand on his own feet as a passionate human being?"[48]

There is no simple answer, and in a complex individual like Johnson, who was both a man of the world and a man of intense religious feeling, the answer was especially elusive because his temperament would not permit him to pursue a middle course. His nature would not allow him to lead a good life and yet admit that perfection was unattainable. Always fearful that he had not done enough to be saved, he drove himself mercilessly to do more rather than risk the possibility of damnation. The question that he was always asking himself and upon which he based *Idler* 88 was: "*Hodie quid egisti*?" What have I done today? And the answer was always the same: "something but not enough." As he observed at the end of this essay, "every man is obliged by the supreme master of the universe to improve all the opportunities of good which are afforded him, and to keep in continual activity such abilities as are bestowed upon him." Such was the moral responsibility that Johnson imposed upon his audience; and to them he granted that "he that has improved the virtue or advanced the happiness of one fellow-creature, he that has ascertained a single moral proposition, or added one useful experiment to natural knowledge, may be contented with his own performance, and, with respect to mortals like himself, may demand, like Augustus, to be dismissed at his departure with applause." Such a moral burden he also imposed upon himself but he never allowed himself to experience the spiritual peace of mind that he conceded to his readers, even though he had fulfilled his own conditions. His response instead was to develop an almost obsessive concern with how best to work out his salvation, and in particular, with how best to make use of the talents and time allotted to him.

10

The parable of the talents had always possessed special significance for Johnson as an expression of the need for each man to make the most of what he had been granted by God.[49] Meditating at the end of *Rambler* 77 on the text from Luke 12:48—"of him, to whom much is given, much shall be required"—Johnson observed, "Those, whom God has favoured with superiour faculties, and made eminent for quickness of intuition, and accuracy of distinctions, will certainly be regarded as culpable in his eye, for defects and deviations which, in souls less enlightened, may be guiltless." And Johnson had realized from an early age, owing largely to the reaction of his parents and teachers, that he did possess remarkable abilities, not the least of which were a near photographic memory, extraordinary powers of concentration, great intellectual curiosity, and an admirable capacity to grasp abstract principles. But he was never content to glory in the temporary fame such faculties earned him; it was necessary to put them to use, to help others, and to promote virtue. It was this conviction, which at times became almost pathological, that was responsible for some of the brightest as well as some of the darkest moments of his life. On the one hand it helped to produce the *Dictionary*, undertaken, as he noted in the "Preface," with "the spirit of a man that has endeavoured well"; but on the other hand it helped to bring on two terrible depressions as well as many moments of agonizing despondency.

The nature of this self-created pressure was such, however, that Johnson was never able to relax and to enjoy what he had accomplished. Even after he received his royal pension, he felt compelled to complete the long-promised work on Shakespeare, to revise the *Dictionary,* and, when he was seventy, to write *The Lives of the Poets.* What was it in his character that drove him to do so much? W. Jackson Bate has argued in his recent majestic biography that this compulsion sprang from a number of deep inner needs to be accepted by family and friends as well as from his profound desire to come to terms with his own expectations of performance and success.[50] And there is much truth in this view. But the obsessive nature of this drive can be fully understood only when we realize that the principal motivation for most of his actions was his desire not so much to fulfil his own expectations as to please God. His deepest need was to feel that he had done everything in his power and at every single moment to do good and to promote virtue. He lived in fear not so much of failing to meet his own exacting standards of achievement as of failing to meet those of God, by which he knew he would finally be judged.

This concern was so intense that it bordered on the self-destructive and was the principal source, as we have seen, of his melancholy. Boswell, in his fine summary of Johnson's character at the end of the *Life,* makes this point most tactfully. "The solemn text, 'of him to whom much is given, much will be required' seems to have been ever present to his mind, in a rigorous sense, and to have made him dissatisfied with his labours and acts of goodness, however comparatively great; so that the unavoidable consciousness of his superiority was, in that respect, a cause of disquiet."[51]

Related to his desire to make the best possible use of his God-given talents was his obsession with time. Convinced that life was at best very short, he was determined to use every moment to do as much good as he could. As he observed in Sermon 15, "the business of life is to work out our salvation; and the days are few in which provision must be made for eternity." He never thought of time except in religious terms, except in terms of the opportunity it afforded him to perform those actions that would find favor with God. This attitude was, of course, inherently destructive since there was no way in which he, or any other individual, could possibly live up to this ideal. But the impossibility of this standard never caused him to question it. On the contrary, he so believed in it—and in its value as an ideal toward which he should aspire—

that he considered any deviation from it as sinful. He considered his indolence, for example, his "reigning sin," largely because of its power to subvert his intention to do good.

The earliest and perhaps most representative example of Johnson's self-destructive fascination with time occurs in the *Life* where Boswell reports that Johnson told a friend, Peter Paradise, that during his breakdown of 1729–30 "he was sometimes so languid and inefficient, that he could not distinguish the hour upon the town-clock."[52] That Johnson, who was then in an acute state of depression, which was in large part produced by his inability to figure out how best to use his time and talents, should remark that he could not tell what time it was is a striking indication of how obsessed he was with time itself. Even in this period of paralyzing lassitude, he was unable to prevent himself from looking at the symbol of what had caused his depression.

This preoccupation deepened as the years passed and as he became acutely conscious of how much time he wasted and of how little remained. It became one of the central themes of the periodical essays, as I shall discuss later, and it is also central to any understanding of *Rasselas,* as Geoffrey Tillotson has shown.[53] But it is in Johnson's own private meditations that we get the deepest sense of how much of his life was spent trying to redeem the hour that was then passing. For to redeem time was to redeem himself.

> September 7, 1738: And O Lord, enable me by thy Grace to use all diligence in redeeming the time which I have spent in Sloth, Vanity, and wickedness; to make use of thy Gifts to the honour of thy Name . . . and finally to obtain everlasting Life. . . .
> January 1, 1748: Almighty and most merciful Father . . . grant that I may so remember my past Life, as to repent of the days and years which I have spent in forgetfulness of thy mercy and neglect of my own Salvation, and so use the time which thou shalt yet allow me, as that I may become every day more diligent in the duties which in thy Providence shall be assigned me. . . .
> Easter Eve. 1757: Enable me to shake off Sloth, and to redeem the time mispent in idleness and Sin by a diligent application of the days yet remaining. . . .
> January 1, 1766: Almighty and most merciful Father, I

> again appear in thy presence the wretched mispender of another year which thy mercy has allowed me. . . . Take not from me thy Holy Spirit but grant that I may redeem the time lost. . . .
> September 18, 1775: O God . . . accept my imperfect thanks for the length of days which thou hast vouchsafed to grant me, impress upon my mind such repentance of the time mispent in sinfulness and negligence, that I may obtain forgiveness of all my offenses.[54]

Given the depth of this feeling, it is no wonder that Johnson inscribed on the dial of a gold watch that he bought in his early fifties the Biblical inscription "the hour cometh when no man can work."

The combined effect of these two convictions was to create in Johnson an intense intellectual and moral seriousness that became one of the distinguishing traits of his character. Convinced that his talents must be well employed and that he had very little time in which to use them, he invested each moment of his life and each action of his life and each action of his life with profound significance. Increasingly he thought of existence as a state of probation in which man seeks not only to avoid evil but to do good, in which man endeavors to "manage" himself as best he can in order to promote virtue and to obtain redemption. "Our time is short, and our work is great: it is therefore with the kindest earnestness enjoined by the apostle that we use all diligence to make our 'calling and election sure'" (Sermon 15).

It is thus not surprising that Johnson came to regard his own work as a professional writer with religious seriousness. As Paul Fussell has rightly perceived, Johnson "conceive[d] of writing as something very like a Christian sacrament, defined in the Anglican catechism as 'an outward and visible sign of an inward and spiritual grace given unto us.'"[55] Although almost all of Johnson's early writing was necessitated by the fear of poverty, and although Johnson continually complained about the difficulties inherent in the process, nevertheless he believed that his writing was the principal professional means by which he could work toward his salvation. He took his work—and indeed all of his intellectual projects—so seriously that he often composed a prayer at the start of one of them. He wrote such a prayer when he began to publish *The Rambler* in 1750 and again in 1752 when he turned to the second volume of the *Dictionary*. On this latter occasion he wrote: "O God who hast hitherto supported me enable me to proceed in this labour & in the Whole task of my present state that when I shall render up at the last day an account of the talent committed to me I may receive pardon for the sake of Jesus Christ."[56] The aim of human life, as Johnson came to understand it, was not only to employ talents and to redeem time but, above all, to work out his salvation, in the literal sense of that phrase. And it was this religious conviction that was Johnson's most profound reaction to his fear that he might waste his life and be damned.

11

Johnson's character, then, was forged on the anvil of anxiety. It was formed in reaction to these three fears—of death, insanity, and misspending his life—each one of which had great power and each one of which, if left unchecked, was capable of plunging Johnson into paralyzing despair. In order to avoid succumbing to such a state, Johnson was forced to develop some defense against such powerful forces, some way in which he could "wrestle" them down and control them. And his response—to immerse himself in life, to analyze the dynamics of the human mind, and to regard every moment of his existence as an opportunity to work toward his salvation—created his character. His reaction to these fears caused Johnson to develop particular convictions and values that formed the core of his being and shaped the nature of his beliefs. Thus his character was at heart religious because most of these fears sprang ultimately from his horror of damnation. His character evolved, then, as a defense against his fear that life was chaotic and meaningless; and as a result it manifested itself most strikingly as a search for sanity and salvation. As he observed in *Rambler* 7, "the great task of him, who conducts his life by the precepts of religion, is to make the future predominate over the present, to impress upon his mind so strong a sense of the importance of obedience to the divine will, of the value of the reward promised to virtue, and the terrors of the punishment denounced against crimes, as may overbear all the temptations which temporal hope or fear can bring in his way."

Johnson was such a man and Johnson sought to conduct

himself in accord with this ideal, but he never managed to do so to his satisfaction. The history of this struggle, intense but largely repressed, expressed itself most significantly in the great moral writing of his middle age, where the conflict between the role he wanted his faith to play and that which he found it could play became all too clear.

5
The Meaning of the Journey

It is the journey, not the arrival, which matters.
Anonymous

The profound tension in Johnson's faith that had become the central preoccupation of his religious faith and that had shaped his character expressed itself as well in the great moral writing that he produced from 1749 to 1759. Desirous of making his faith the center of his life but fearful that he would not be able to do so to his satisfaction, Johnson had begun seriously to question the meaning of life's journey. Ever since his religion had become "the predominant object of his thoughts," he had conceived of life as a spiritual pilgrimage in which he, like Christian in *Pilgrim's Progress* (one of Johnson's three favorite books), sought to resist earthly temptations and to seek eternal life. But his own journey had caused him to doubt if he could ever achieve sufficient self-mastery to attain redemption as well as to wonder if the essential "misery of life" could be alleviated by faith in a divinely ordered world.

What Johnson had begun to question was the degree to which the Christian view of life provided the most satisfactory explanation for the pain and sorrow that he increasingly felt were inherent in human existence. What he feared to admit was that life might be meaningless and that all efforts to understand it were doomed by definition to failure. This growing fear created in Johnson a terrible conflict between his need to believe in the efficacy of the Christian faith and his fear that it could not provide the direction, meaning, and peace of mind that he sought. He felt himself torn between the role that he wanted his faith to play and that which he increasingly feared it could not perform. And it was this conflict that constituted his principal concern in the great decade of moral writing that began with *The Vanity of Human Wishes*, that included the periodical essays, and that culminated in the enigmatic conclusion to *Rasselas*. At stake was not only his *raison d'être* but above all his sanity.

2

Nowhere did Johnson give a clearer indication of the role he wanted religion to play in human existence than at the end of *The Vanity of Human Wishes*.[1] After his devastating survey of human aspiration and frustration, Johnson asks in three powerful couplets the inevitable question:

> Where then shall Hope and Fear their objects find?
> Must dull Suspence corrupt the stagnant mind?
> Must helpless man, in ignorance sedate,
> Roll darkling down the torrent of his fate?
> Must no dislike alarm, no wishes rise,
> No cries attempt the mercies of the skies?

If man cannot find lasting happiness in wealth, power, fame, or grandeur, where then will he find it? And Johnson's response is clear, direct, and even more impersonal than he had been elsewhere in the poem. "Enquirer, cease, petitions yet remain, / Which heav'n may hear, nor deem religion vain." As W. J. Bate has pointed out, "Johnson, who had himself been the questioner, suddenly puts the questioner at a distance by addressing him as though he were another person."[2] The effect of this strategy is to depersonalize the tone of what follows and to emphasize the general argument made for the value of religion in human life.

By religion, Johnson means an undefined combination of submission to the divine will and prayer, a mysterious synthesis of surrender and supplication. ("Still raise for good the supplicating voice, / But leave to heav'n the measure and the choice.") Juvenal had recommended much the same sort of balance in the original poem and had expressed his conviction that every man had within himself the power to stand in such a relationship to the Deity and so to lead a happy and virtuous life. (*"Monstro quod ipse tibi possis dare."*) But Johnson, as he drew near to the end of his own poem, chose to emphasize not self-reliance but rather man's profound dependence upon God for any possibility of happiness.

And this complete dependence was most fully achieved in the act of prayer, which Johnson defined "as a reposal of myself upon God and a resignation of all into his holy hand." Through prayer man could create for himself a state of mind that would be ultimately conducive to spiritual peace.

At this point, where he suggests specific objects of prayer, Johnson departs even more substantially from Juvenal. His first three recommended objects—"a healthy mind, / Obedient passions, and a will resign'd"—are initially faithful to the original but then are subsumed and utterly changed by the second triad—"for love . . . for patience . . . for faith." Here Johnson's ambivalence to the Stoic creed gives way under the pressure of his own Christian belief and brings about a substitution in which two of the most important Stoic values—"*mens sana in corpore sano*" and "*animum fortem*"—are replaced by a triad that springs with only slight variation from Corinthians 1:13. In so doing, Johnson dramatizes his conviction that Christianity is a meaningful answer to the existential morass that he had described earlier in the poem. These are the "goods" that man should pray for; and these are the "goods" that the Christian God can confer upon the true believer, thereby granting him a spiritual peace of mind that he has never known before. "With these [goods] celestial wisdom calms the mind, / And makes the happiness she does not find."

Most readers of the poem have found these final lines to be a logical and moving conclusion to the poem as a whole. Sir John Hawkins noted long ago that "the poem concludes with an answer to an enquiry that must necessarily result from the perusal of the foregoing part of it, viz. what are the consolations that human life affords? or, in other words, in whom or on what is a virtuous man to rest his hope? The resolution of this question is contained in the following lines, which for dignity of sentiment, for pious instruction, and purity of style, are hardly to be equalled by any in our language."[3] And most critics since have concurred with this judgment. Mary Lascelles, for example, has observed that "Johnson approaches the final question—'what may we then implore?'—without ironic overtones" and proceeds to amplify his answer in such a way that it "is consistent with the course of his argument in this poem."[4]

Most attention in recent years, however, has centered less on what Sir Walter Scott called "the deep and pathetick morality of the poem" and more on the way Johnson's own Christian beliefs transformed the Stoicism of Juvenal into what F. W. Hilles has described as Johnson's "fundamental philosophy of life, what has been termed Christian Stoicism."[5] The editors of the Yale edition of the poem have argued that "the ending of *The Vanity of Human Wishes* is a good example of how Johnson's own ideas transformed his source. Juvenal's conclusion is nobly ethical, Stoical at basis, whereas Johnson's is deeply religious, bringing the poem to a close conformable with his own nature."[6] And Leopold Damrosch has agreed with this point of view and then argued that "Johnson intended his Christian ending as a kind of *tour de force,* answering the despair of the classical poet with the truth of revelation, and making the happiness he could not find."[7] But these arguments for the internal logic and emotional power of the conclusion do not hold up under close study of the text. These last lines do express Johnson's answer to the question posed in the poem but it is an inadequate and unconvincing response.

The answer that Johnson gives, namely, to resign oneself to the divine will, is, of course, a familiar and traditional response of the religious man to these timeless questions. But as Johnson frames it here it is peculiarly flat and insipid.

> Enquirer, cease, petitions yet remain,
> Which heav'n may hear, nor deem religion vain.
> Still raise for good the supplicating voice,
> But leave to heav'n the measure and the choice,
> Safe in his pow'r whose eyes discern afar
> The secret ambush of a specious pray'r.
> Implore his aid, in his decisions rest,
> Secure whate'er he gives, he gives the best.

As this passage stands, it is an assertion of Johnson's belief in the value of religion rather than a demonstration of its worth. The repeated use of the imperative—"cease," "raise," "leave," "implore," "rest," and "rescue"—creates a sense of authority and urgency but cannot conceal what is essentially a conventional argument. The final couplet of the passage quoted above illustrates especially well this problem. The syntactical balance of the first line—"implore his aid, in his decisions rest"—reasserts the relationship between supplication and resignation that Johnson had been discussing in the preceding six lines. But the second half of the couplet adds nothing and falls into airy generality—"secure whate'er he gives, he gives the best."

This latter phrase is especially startling because it appears to pay more than lip service to a facile conception of divinity that Johnson associated with Pope in *The Essay on Man* and that he would soon excoriate in his review of Soame Jenyns's *A Free Inquiry* (1757). His objection in both cases was the ease with which Pope and Jenyns dismissed the problem of evil and the reality of human suffering by citing the insufficiency of human knowledge regarding the divine plan. We can hear real anger in Johnson's voice when toward the end of the review he wrote: "The only end of writing is to enable the readers better to enjoy life, or better to endure it: and how will either of those be put more in our power by him who tells us that we are puppets, of which some creature not much wiser than ourselves manages the wires. That a set of beings unseen and unheard, are hovering about us, trying experiments upon our sensibility, putting us in agonies to see our limbs quiver, torturing us to madness, that they may laugh at our vagaries, sometimes obstructing the bile, that they may see how a man looks when he is yellow."[8]

We know from Johnson's numerous remarks in the *Life* and from his notations in his private meditations that he had a much more complex and *fearful* conception of how God governed the universe than he reveals in this shallow assertion that "he gives the best." We have already seen how hard he struggled to reconcile his image of God as the benevolent Father with that of God as "the implacable Judge." We have already observed how much Johnson feared that the divine system of justice was not as perfect as it ought to have been. And we have already heard of the various doubts Johnson experienced regarding his own spiritual condition. Thus this bland assertion stands at odds with all that we know about what Johnson believed and all that we know about the way he conducted his religious life. How, then, can we explain this rather uninspired conclusion to an otherwise great poem?

The reasons for this tension are complex since they relate both to literary and to psychological values of Johnson. To start, Johnson was almost certainly inhibited by his desire to remain faithful to the spirit, if not the letter, of Juvenal's Stoic conclusion. Johnson defined imitation in the *Dictionary* as "a method of translating looser than paraphrase, in which modern examples and illustrations are used for ancient, or domestick for foreign." This had been his practice when twelve years before he had written *London* in imitation of Juvenal's third satire. His respect for the form of the original had been such then that he had instructed the publisher to print the corresponding passages of Juvenal at the bottom of the page since he felt that "part of the beauty of the performance . . . [consists] in adapting Juvenal's sentiments to modern facts and persons."[9] He was not so strict in this regard when he published *The Vanity of Human Wishes* since he omitted the original lines but he still stuck closely to the sentiment and style of the model.

This adherence did not pose much of a problem for Johnson in the bulk of the poem, largely because, as Ian Jack has observed, Johnson found in Juvenal "at once a somber reading of life which had much in common with his own and an object lesson in the art of impressing what he had to say on the minds of his readers."[10] But in the conclusion, where Juvenal's Stoicism emerges clearly, Johnson found it more difficult to sustain the philosophic spirit of the original, in part because of his distrust of this school of thought and in part because of the strength of his own Christian beliefs. Johnson was torn between his desire to respect the argument of the original and his equally strong desire to assert his belief in the efficacy of the Christian faith.

Second, Johnson may well have possessed at this time some of the same reservations regarding the expression of religious sentiment in poetry that he later recorded in *The Life of Waller*. He made clear there that he felt there was no way in which poetry could add to the force and truth of religious ideas. "The ideas of Christian Theology are too simple for eloquence, too sacred for fiction, and too majestick for ornament." But he was quick to add that "doctrines of religion may indeed be defended in a didactick poem; and he who has the happy power of arguing in verse, will not lose it because his subject is sacred."[11] One side of Johnson clearly felt that the innate magnitude of religion made it an impossible subject to treat properly in poetry. But another side of him acknowledged that religion might indeed be included in a poem that sought to instruct. It is hard, moreover, not to believe that Johnson had the end of *The Vanity of Human Wishes* in mind when he made this concession, since the remark describes the way Johnson used religion in a poem that is clearly didactic. Thus the ambivalence implicit in these remarks may well have restrained Johnson from giving full expression to his own religious convictions. But there was a deeper conflict at work within

Johnson, which he had been unable to resolve and which could no longer be contained.

Johnson, as we have already observed, had a deep psychological need to believe in a religious view of life as well as an equally demanding need to provide a rational basis for that belief. This passionate "will to believe," to use William James's well-known phrase, sprang ultimately from his sense of man's lonely and uncertain condition—"Must helpless man in ignorance sedate, / Roll darkling down the torrent of his fate?"—and from his instinctive conviction that the most satisfactory way to endure that condition was to place our trust in a divinely ordered universe—"Still raise for good the supplicating voice, / But leave to heav'n the measure and the choice." He wanted his faith, in the words of Alfred North Whitehead, to become "the central element in a coherent ordering of life."[12]

Working against this desire, however, was the fear that the religious solution to the riddle of life was inadequate. It provided neither a satifactory explanation for the misery of existence nor a convincing demonstration that it was the sole path to happiness. On the contrary, Johnson had been forced to conclude from his own experience that the attempt to conduct one's life in accord with one's religious beliefs was more often than not a cause of great personal unhappiness and anxiety. At its best, religion could provide genuine solace but little more; it could relieve what he once called "the pain of being a man" but it could not eradicate that pain. In turning to Juvenal's great poem and in composing his own version of it, Johnson recognized more fully than he ever had before the extent to which all men in all times had expressed the same hopes and had experienced the same disappointments. He realized, furthermore, that there was no way in which this pattern of expectation and frustration could be reversed or remedied. It was beyond man's control; it was in the nature of things, in the nature of human life. This had been the main point of his own survey of human history.

But a terrible question remained. If life could offer no lasting satisfaction or happiness, how then could man enjoy or endure it? And it was at this point that Johnson, following the example of Juvenal, gave the response that he wanted to believe was true rather than the one he feared was true. He had staked his life upon the belief that existence had meaning, namely, as an attempt to obey the divine will and to regain God's grace, and he was reluctant to surrender that conviction out of fear of the personal chaos that would inevitably arise. As a result he drafted a response that was loyal to the spirit of Juvenal's Stoicism and yet still expressive of what he wanted to believe. He still wanted to believe that religion could calm the mind and provide substantial happiness, but he was less certain of this conviction than he had once been, owing to his own experience and to his increased understanding of the forces within himself and within the world over which he had little or no control. This tension, implicit in the end of the poem, became explicit in the moral writing that followed in the ensuing decade.

3

In the great moral writing that appeared in the periodical essays, Johnson continued to explore the central question of his major poem but from a different perspective. Johnson's principal concern became not so much to record notable examples of the essential futility of human aspiration as to discover the origins of the forces in the mind that give rise to this tragic pattern of desire and frustration. His interest had become less historical and more psychological, less didactic and more moral. Having dramatized the effects of such forces, he now sought to understand their origin. He no longer wanted to know where hope and fear would find their objects but instead how man could control such passions and put them to use in a life of virtue. He had come to realize that if man could not attain sufficient mastery of himself and of the forces that determined his conduct, he had no real hope for salvation. The pressure of this realization inspired him to make his extraordinary dissection of the human mind.

The human psyche, as Johnson understood it, was a dynamic, restless, and insatiable force that abhorred stasis and thrived on activity, even when that activity was meaningless and destructive. As he observed at the end of *Rambler* 6, "such are the vicissitudes of the world, through all its parts, that day and night, labour and rest, hurry and retirement, endear each other; such are the changes that keep the mind in action; we desire, we pursue, we obtain, we are satiated; we desire something else, and begin a new persuit." Each individual had to acknowledge the existence of these forces, which could not be destroyed but could be governed. As Johnson remarked in *Rambler* 151, "nature will indeed always operate, human desires will be always ranging; but these motions, though very powerful, are not resistless; nature may be regulated, and desires governed; and to contend with the predominance of successive passions, to be endangered first by one affection, and then by another, is the condition upon which we are to pass our time, the time of our preparation for that state which shall put an end to experiment, to disappointment, and to change."

Man cannot eliminate or escape from the frustration and suffering that is inherent in human life, but he can learn—and must learn for his own well-being—how to live with it. As he wrote in *Rambler* 32, "the controversy about the reality of external evils is now at an end. That life has many miseries, and that those miseries are, sometimes at least, equal to all the powers of fortitude, is now universally confessed; and therefore it is useful to consider not only how we may escape them, but by what means . . . [they] may be mitigated and lightened." And this became his chief concern in the periodical essays that he wrote during the 1750s. His chief end, as he declared in *Rambler* 11, was "the regulation of common life," or as he stated in *Rambler* 8, "the moral discipline of the mind."

Johnson believed that there were two principal means by which man could learn how to manage his mind in such a way as to produced a life of virtue. The first was rational. Through the use of reason man could understand the complex psychological forces that shaped his character and determined his conduct. By acquiring such insight, he could then lead what Sir Philip Sidney once called "the life of virtuous action" and in that way prepare to work out his salvation. As Johnson explained in *Rambler* 8: "he therefore that would govern his actions by the laws of virtue, must regulate his thoughts by those of reason; he must keep guilt from the recesses of his heart, and remember that the pleasures of fancy, and the emotions of desire, are more dangerous as they are more hidden, since they escape the awe of observation, and operate equally in every situation, without the concurrence of external opportunities." Reason, then, had the power both to detect the insidious ways in which our passions misled us and to redirect them in such a way that a virtuous life was possible. Johnson was never very clear about how reason operated in this anguished tug-of-war, but he was insistent about its power to reveal to all men "the true motives of action" and the true end of life. Reason showed man the limits of his own nature as well as those of his own expectations. And, above all, it reminded him that the ultimate end of life was not the pursuit of earthly achievement but the working out of our salvation. Johnson made this point clear when he remarked in *Rambler* 127 that all our errors "arise from an original mistake of the true motives of action. He that never extends his view beyond the praises or rewards of men, will be dejected by neglect and envy, or infatuated by honours and applause. But the consideration that life is only deposited in his hands to be employed in obedience to a Master who will regard his endeavours, not his success, would have preserved him from trivial elations and discouragements, and enabled him to proceed with constancy and chearfulness, neither enervated by commendation, nor intimidated by censure."

Implicit in these remarks is Johnson's conviction that the other important way to moderate our passions and to pursue virtuous ends was to remind ourselves of our religious condition. Reason could not always triumph over what he called "the hunger of the imagination," and stronger measures were necessary to insure the victory of virtue. Such measures were at heart religious as they all aimed to shift man's attention from himself to God and as they all sought to transfer man's hopes from this life to the next by fear of divine punishment and by hope of divine reward. And it was these measures that Johnson had in mind when he claimed in the last *Rambler* that all of these essays "will be found exactly conformable to the precepts of Christianity."

There were three primary measures, all intimately related to each other, that Johnson held up again and again in the periodical essays—and indeed in his own private meditations—as incentives to virtue. First, he advocated, as in *Rambler* 17, frequent reflection upon the shortness of life. "The known shortness of life, as it ought to moderate our passions, may likewise, with equal propriety, contract our designs." The main purpose of such reflection was not so much to remind man of the brevity of existence as it was to exhort him to make the most of the time left to him. His deepest concern was not with length of life but with the lost opportunity to do what good we can and thus to please God. As he remarked in *Rambler* 134, "the certainty that life cannot be long, and the probability that it will be much shorter than nature allows, ought to awaken every man to the active prosecution of whatever he is desirous to perform." And since Johnson was convinced that man's deepest satisfaction sprang from his hope for salvation, it was not surprising that he became, as we have seen, obsessed by "the silent celerity of time." For it was through time that man would work out his salvation.

Despite his well-known fear of death, Johnson advocated the contemplation of death as another effective way to induce man to pursue a virtuous life. He noted in *Rambler* 17: "A frequent and attentive prospect of that moment, which must put a period to all our schemes, and deprive us of all our acquisitions, is indeed, of the utmost efficacy to the just and rational regulation of our lives: nor would ever anything wicked, or often anything absurd, be undertaken or prosecuted by him who should begin every day with a serious reflection, that he is born to die." The thought of death was for Johnson an important check upon our endless propensity to create new schemes and to engage in foolish or wicked actions. It reminded man of how little time he had to establish his worth in the eyes of God as well as how near that moment of divine judgment was. "The great incentive to virtue is the reflection that we must die; it will therefore be useful to accustom ourselves, whenever we see a funeral, to consider how soon we may be added to the number of those whose probation is past, and whose happiness or misery shall endure forever." To think on death for Johnson meant to think on life—on how we can best live it. And he could not reflect upon this life without inevitably seeing it as a preparation for a future life, for that life after death promised by the Christian faith. It was this view of existence that impelled Johnson to remark pointedly to Boswell, "it matters not how a man dies but how he lives."

Finally, Johnson believed that frequent reflection upon the fundamental uncertainty of life would awaken in all men the desire to do as much good as they could today rather than to defer such effort until tomorrow. He believed, furthermore, that all men shared this conviction of life's uncertainty and that most of them recognized that it sprang mainly from their inability to determine either the length of their lives or the time of their deaths. "We cannot doubt the uncertainty," he remarked in *Adventurer* 108, when "we see every day the unexpected death of our friends and our enemies, [when] we see new graves hourly opened for men older and younger than ourselves, for the cautious and the careless, the dissolute and the temperate, for men who like us were providing to enjoy or improve hours now irreversibly cut off." He recognized that most men who acknowledged the universality of this condition often ignored its obvious consequences, refusing to believe that their lives would end before they had planned or that they might lack sufficient strength of will to achieve their goals. "We are so unwilling to believe any thing to our own disadvantage, that we always imagine the perspicacity of our judgment and the strength of our resolution more likely to increase than to grow less by time; and, therefore, conclude that the will to persue laudable purpose will be always seconded by the power." In spite of man's tendency to deceive himself in calculating the strength of his faculties, Johnson asserted at the end of this essay that "it is our duty to struggle" to subdue this unwillingness; for "surely, nothing is more unworthy of a reasonable being, than to shut his eyes, when he sees the road which he is commanded to travel, that he deviate with fewer reproaches from himself." The implication of Johnson's argument is clear. Man has a moral responsibility to use each moment of his life to promote virtue and he must not avert his eyes from any measure that would help him attain this end, even if it causes him pain.

These were the principal measures that Johnson recommended to insure the promotion of virtue and the increase of piety. He still believed that the religious explanation of the meaning of life provided the best solution to the riddle of existence. It was still what he wanted to believe; it was still "the highest perfection of humanity"; it was still the basis for all human conduct. As he remarked in *Rambler* 185, "the utmost excellence at which humanity can arrive, is a constant and determinate pursuit of virtue, without regard to present dangers or advantage; a continued reference of every action to the divine will; an habitual appeal to everlasting justice; and an unvaried elevation of the intellectual eye to the reward which perseverance only can obtain." He had, however, adopted a new attitude about the way in which man might most effectively attain this "utmost excellence." He had come to realize that he could not simply declare that "whate'er he [God] gives, he gives the best," nor could he simply urge man to "leave to heav'n the measure and the choice." He must demonstrate how trust in God helps man to assuage his anxiety about his uncertain and troubled existence. He must make clear how religious faith provides the most substantial answer to man's acute sense of the misery of life. It was this realization that had impelled Johnson to undertake his analysis of the human psyche. He knew that if man did not understand the nature of these powerful forces and how they worked, then he could never hope to learn how to control them so that learning, virtue, and piety might be increased. Johnson thus recognized that man's happiness depended not only upon his capacity for faith but also upon his willingness to submit himself to a moral discipline that would enable him to work out his salvation. Herein lay man's hope for happiness.

Working against this hope, however, were two substantial fears that Johnson had encountered in his inquiry into the nature of the human mind and that had seriously shaken his confidence in the power of faith to provide life with meaning. First, Johnson was haunted by the possibility that the mind was in essence uncontrollable, hostile to truth, and treacherous. Even though he asserted on numerous occasions man's ability to "regulate" his passions and arrive at self-knowledge, still he was unable to dispel his fear that the mind could never be truly ordered. He had been forced to accept the fact that the whispers of the imagination frequently triumphed over the dictates of reason and that the pursuit of pleasure was usually more appealing than the quest for truth. At the heart of this fear was Johnson's belief that if man could not discipline himself he could never achieve a full sense of his responsibility to himself and to others. Like Pope and Swift before him, Johnson cherished self-knowledge and self-control as indispensable qualities for the moral conduct of life. And it was the force of this concern that made Johnson the last of the Augustans.

Second, Johnson now realized more clearly than ever before the degree to which human happiness was not only unknowable in this life but also uncertain in the life to come. In *Rambler* 203, after reviewing some of the means by which man seeks to perpetuate the pleasures he has known on earth, Johnson dismisses these efforts as vain and urges his reader to place his hope instead in the Christian notion of immortality. "It is not therefore from this world, that any ray of comfort can proceed to cheer the gloom of the last hour. But futurity has still its prospects; there is yet happiness in reserve, which if we transfer our attention to it, will support us in the pains of disease, and the languor of decay. This happiness we may expect with confidence, because it is out of the power of chance, and may be attained by all that sincerely and earnestly pursue it. On this therefore every man ought finally to rest. Hope is the chief blessing of man, and that hope only is rational, of which we are certain that it cannot deceive us."

This exhortation is deeply moving but it is not entirely convincing because there is no reason for Johnson to believe, other than his faith in the goodness of God, that this religious hope will prove any more realizable than many secular aspirations. For in all of his writing about hope at this time, Johnson was always quick to affirm man's need to hope but equally quick to warn of the disappointment and frustration that ensued. As he observed in *Rambler* 67, "hope is necessary in every condition. The miseries of poverty, of sickness, of captivity, would, without this comfort, be insupportable." But hope is also "very fallacious" as it raises expectations that are seldom, if ever, met. It thus often "promises what it seldom gives, though its promises are more valuable than the gifts of fortune" because hope "seldom frustrates us without assuring us of recompensing the delay by a greater bounty." But there is, of course, no assurance that this "greater bounty" will not also prove unsatisfying in its turn. In short, there is, no more reason to place one's trust in the hope of immortality than in the possibility of everlasting fame. This suspicion, combined with his fear of the unmanageable quality of the mind, haunted Johnson when he wrote *Rasselas.*

4

The traditional interpretation of *Rasselas* has been that it is the fullest expression of Johnson's tragic view of life, of man's ill-fated quest for human happiness. As such, it derives from Boswell's remark that "Johnson meant, by shewing the unsatisfactory nature of things temporal, to direct the hopes of man to things eternal."[13] In modern times, Gwin Kolb has been the most articulate spokesman of this point of view. Here is the essence of his reading of the tale: "Human limitations make happiness in this world ephemeral, accidental, the product of hope rather than reality, and almost as nothing compared to the miseries of life; consequently, searches for permanent enjoyment, although inevitable to man as man, are bound to end in failure. The wise man, therefore, will accept submissively the essential grimness of life; seek no more lasting felicity than is given by a quiet conscience, and live with an eye to eternity, in which he may perhaps find, through the mercy of God, the complete happiness unattainable on earth."[14] Writing largely in reaction to this long-held view, Alvin Whitley has described *Rasselas* "not primarily as a positive statement of Johnson's philosophy" but rather as "a satire on the illusioned view of life."[15] As he sees it, its spirit is comic and satiric; it is in essence a comedy of ideas in which Johnson ridicules particular theories of life that are supposed to bring happiness and contentment. The comedy itself arises in part from the naivete of the travelers themselves, in part from the objects and the ideas they view, and in part from the reaction of the travelers to what they encounter.

Neither of these interpretations is satisfactory. The tragic fails because while there are numerous examples in the tale of Johnson's belief in "the unsatisfactory nature of things temporal," there is no explicit or implicit evidence for his desire "to direct the hopes of man to things eternal." It is not a simple matter of cause and effect. It cannot be argued that because the travelers do not find lasting happiness on earth, Johnson meant to imply that such happiness can be found only in heaven. The text itself offers no support for this view; in strict point of fact it argues against such a position. In chapters 47 and 48 Johnson had two opportunities through Imlac to make a persuasive case for the religious view of life and in both instances he chose not to do so. In the debate on the virtues of the monastic life with Nekayah, Imlac not only refuses to decide whether a monk is more holy than "he that lives well in the world" but also declines to argue for a life led in strict accord with such principles. And in the following chapter in the visit to the catacombs, Imlac chooses to deliver a discourse on the soul that leaves his listeners confused and bored—Nekayah even remarks "I know not any great use of this question"—rather than a meditation on the significance of a religious life. Although Rasselas is led momentarily to reflect on the shortness of life and Nekayah on "the choice of eternity," nevertheless these thoughts are fleeting, as the last chapter makes clear. The religious approach to life has been considered and rejected by the travelers as one more choice of life that ultimately provides no more happiness than any other pursuit.

The comic view of *Rasselas* is also inadequate because although it provides a plausible explanation for two-thirds of the tale, for those episodes in which particular philosophies of life like the Stoic and the Hedonistic are satirized, nevertheless such an approach does not do justice to the last third of the tale, where the travelers experience the sorrows of life for themselves. The abduction of Pekuah, the meetings with the mad astronomer, and the encounter with the old man cannot be treated as "dark comedy." For each episode concerns the possible loss of something that Johnson considered indispensable in the search for human happiness—the loss of a friend, the loss of reason, the loss of hope. In each case he treats this loss with sympathy, while emphasizing the degree to which human life is subject to bad luck, accidents, and forces beyond our control. Johnson's purpose was not primarily to ridicule Nekayah's excessive grief at the kidnapping of Pekuah, nor to satirize the smug and insensitive reaction of the ladies to the mad astronomer and the old man, nor finally to mock the ongoing search for happiness. To laugh at these things was to make fun of life itself and that Johnson could not do. This comic view of *Rasselas* is inadequate in the end because it refuses to acknowledge that Johnson wants to affirm something about the nature of human life and the quest for human happiness.

What Johnson wished to affirm at the end of *Rasselas* was an absurdist view of life. This view emerged most clearly in the final chapter, which Johnson entitled "The Conclusion in Which Nothing Is Concluded." The illogic of the title is Johnson's first warning to the reader that he must not expect the traditional ending of an oriental tale, where the narrative is neatly tied up and the moral is firmly drawn. And this warning should be heeded because neither the narrative that follows nor the moral that emerges is what we would have expected. In a manner reminiscent of Sterne, Johnson plays upon our formal and moral expectations only to undercut them in order to make his ultimate point more forcefully.

In the concluding narrative, Johnson quickly relates how the inundation of the Nile forced the travelers to retire indoors, where they "diverted themselves with comparisons of the different forms of life which they had observed, and with various schemes of happiness which each of them had formed." He then in three short paragraphs summarizes the respective schemes of happiness that each traveler would choose: Pekuah would retire to a convent; Nekayah would found a college for women; Rasselas would rule a little kingdom; while Imlac and the astronomer (who had regained his sanity) "were contented to be driven along the stream of life without directing their course to any particular port." All of these choices are sensible and the tale itself seems to have reached a plausible conclusion. It would seem that each one of the travelers had decided on the basis of his experience that this new choice of life would provide as much happiness and satisfaction as could be found in the world. But the tale does not end here. There remains one additional paragraph in which Johnson obscures the clarity of the conclusion by nullifying the particular choices of the travelers and by falling into apparent ambiguity. "Of these wishes that they had formed they well knew that none could be obtained. They deliberated a while what was to be done, and resolved, when the inundation should cease, to return to Abissinia." What did Johnson hope to accomplish by this critical reversal of our narrative expectations?

He intended to dramatize that the travelers had at last realized that there was no single choice of life that could be made to satisfy any of them. The nature of desire made such happiness impossible. But Johnson also meant to affirm his belief that man must not abandon his quest for happiness. On the contrary, for man to remain healthy, productive, and sane, he must continue his quest. And this is the absurd predicament in which the travelers find themselves at the end of this tale. They recognize that their most recent choices of life will never be attained but they also know that they have no realistic choice but to continue their journey. As Earl Wasserman has put it, "the ultimate absurdity of life is that one must project the hope of earthly happiness in order to keep going and avoid stagnation, but one must have the educative experience to know that such hopes are in vain and can never be fulfilled."[16] Seeing their dilemma clearly, these travelers make the only possible sensible decision: they resolve to return to Abyssinia. Now much critical attention has been devoted to this famous crux and all in vain; for given the absurd conclusion that the travelers have been forced to accept about human life, it does not matter whether they return to the Happy Valley or to Abyssinia. In either place they will find themselves trapped in the same dilemma that they encountered in the world.

In either place they will discover that in order to avoid stagnation, boredom, and despair they must surrender to the tyranny of hope and to the illusion of happiness.

This is the meaning of Johnson's conclusion. Man has no choice but to hope and be disappointed, to seek happiness that will never be found. He must accept the truth that life cannot be fully ordered or entirely understood. To borrow two of the central images that Johnson employs in this final chapter, life is a stream along which we are driven by a variety of forces, some of which we can understand and control and some of which we will never understand and never control. And life is also a journey in which we hope to arrive at a preconceived destination of happiness only to discover that we seem never to arrive. We may travel but we never arrive. Thus, as Emrys Jones has observed, this is "an ending in which 'the choice of life' is not decided, a decision that nothing can end here, a decision that nothing can be simply decided, and an ending that acknowledges the seeming endlessness of things."[17]

It is also an ending in which Johnson does not try to console us by offering a religious view of life. There is no suggestion that man should seek solace for the transparent misery of life by hoping for ultimate happiness in some future life. The burden of this conclusion—and indeed of the entire tale as I read it—is that man should not rely on the hope of immortality to endure the pains and uncertainty of existence. And thus I cannot accept the argument of Patrick O'Flaherty that "the paradox of *Rasselas* is that in it an absurdist view of human life is not seen as irreconcilable with the idea of a supervising Divinity."[18] It is true, as he demonstrates, that there are a certain number of references to such a Deity, but they stop as of chapter 34 and are conspicuously absent from the last third of the tale. Thus the image we receive of this Deity is somewhat vague; it is not a force to be considered at the end of the narrative. More importantly, Johnson did not argue, as I pointed out earlier, for the power of religion to relieve existential pain at the place where we would have most expected him to do so, namely, in the visit of the travelers to the catacombs that precedes the final chapter. The point should be clear: no paradox of the sort O'Flaherty describes exists in *Rasselas* because Johnson does not hold up "the idea of a supervising Deity" as the principal means by which to endure life. What Johnson does affirm in *Rasselas* is that man's best hope for overcoming the fundamental absurdity of life is to commit himself once again to the current of the world. It is to return to the stream of life; it is to continue the journey. For as the episode of the astronomer demonstrates, it is only through renewed contact with human life that man is able to regain his sanity and to rediscover the pleasures of existence.

The absurdist view of life that Johnson expressed in *Rasselas* represents a radical change in his habitual confidence in the power of religion to give life its ultimate meaning. It is a dramatic departure from the claims that he explicitly made for religion at the end of *The Vanity of Human Wishes.* Where he once urged man "to leave to heav'n the measure and the choice," he now exhorted man to take charge of his own destiny and of his own quest for earthly happiness. This view is also an important departure from the measures that he implicitly recommended to promote virtue and piety in the periodical essays. Where he once argued strenuously for the need to establish a moral discipline of the mind, he now felt it was just as important for man to involve himself in the ebb and flow of existence. Johnson seems to have lost his trust in the ability of faith to provide a substantial explanation for the riddle of life and to have decided that only by willingly committing oneself to the absurd quest for happiness can one hope to arrive and indeed to survive. Man will not find such happiness here on earth but he must look for it all the same. This is the essence of his absurd predicament.

5

We must be careful, however, not to accept the conclusion of *Rasselas* as Johnson's last word on the place of religion in human life since at the same time he was rejecting religion here he was deriving consolation from it elsewhere. In *Idler* 41, written during the same week as *Rasselas* and inspired by the death of his mother, Johnson, after dismissing the philosophy of the Stoics for its failure to "assuage" human sorrow, wrote a moving apologia to the power of the Christian faith to provide solace. "Real alleviation of the loss of friends, and rational tranquility in the prospect of our own dissolution, can be received only from the promises of him in whose hands are life and death, and from the assurance of another and better state, in which all tears will be wiped from the eyes, and the whole soul shall be filled with joy. Philosophy may infuse stubborness, but religion only can give patience." Johnson has clearly not abandoned his confidence in the power of faith to provide consolation. One powerful side of him still believed that Christianity provided a substantial solution to the misery of life. It could still calm the mind and confer upon the heart a rare serenity. But how do we account for the simultaneous existence of these opposing views?

We must recognize that they dramatize an emerging crisis in Johnson's religious life. He was increasingly torn between his desire to make his faith, as Law had advocated long ago, "the rule and measure of all the actions of ordinary life" and his fear that he could not do so, owing to all that he had learned about how difficult it was to "manage" the mind and how impossible it was to determine the meaning of life. He was further torn between his desire to believe that the Christian view of life offered the only meaningful explanation of existence and his fear that this view was inadequate, if not invalid. Implicit in this latter tension was his greatest fear, namely, that life was meaningless. These tensions had been implicit in the earlier writing at the end of *The Vanity of Human Wishes* and in many of the moral essays. But Johnson did not fully face their implications until early in 1759, when, as Patrick O'Flaherty has suggested, "His horrible suspicion of the essential insignificance of life emerged" into open conflict with his deep need to believe that life did have religious significance. Despite the depth of his personal anguish and despite the power of his suspicion, Johnson refused to abandon his faith. He refused to see life as an absurd quest for ephemeral happiness and he reaffirmed his conviction that it was at heart a long, agonizing journey in search of salvation. That he did so, under such tremendous pressure, is perhaps the strongest indication that we have of his psychological need to believe in a religious *raison d'être.* But this resolution was not perfect; this victory was not complete. The bleak vision of human life expressed in *Rasselas* remained an important part of him and, along with his other doubts and fears, helped to plunge him into the second great depression of his life.

6

A Crisis of Faith

There can hardly have been many so completely at sea in their solitude as he was or so horribly aware of it. Read the Prayers and Meditations if you don't believe me . . . she [Mrs. Thrale] had none of that need to suffer or necessity for suffering that he had.

Samuel Beckett to Thomas McGreevy

This crisis manifested itself as a gradual nervous breakdown that began in 1760 and continued until at least 1767. Johnson himself said almost nothing about what he was experiencing at this time to his friends, with the exception of Dr. Adams and the Thrales, with the result that none of those closest to him were aware that he had sunk into a terrible depression. There were no outward signs to indicate that he was unhappy or to suggest that he felt inner unrest. Boswell, in his account of the early 1760s, did note that Johnson "certainly at this time was not active" in literature and that he wrote fewer letters to his friends than had been his custom.[1] But he was quick to point out that Johnson did write a number of short pieces—prefaces, dedications, and reviews—and he assumed that Johnson must have been busy with his edition of Shakespeare, though he admitted that he had no evidence to support this notion. There did not thus appear on the surface of Johnson's life any indications of emotional distress.

Johnson's notations in his private journals for these years, however, make clear that he was suffering from something far more serious than chronic indolence. He felt anxious and depressed; he was convinced that he had wasted most of his life; and he was more deeply afflicted than ever before by religious doubt. Here is his entry for Easter Eve, 1761: "Since the Communion of last Easter I have led a life so dissipated and useless, and my terrours and perplexities have so much encreased, that I am under great depression and discouragement, yet I purpose to present myself before God tommorow with humble hope that he will not break the bruised reed."[2] The usual resolves follow. The form of the meditation is familiar but the tone is not. As he thinks back over the past year, he is aware that he has lost what little self-control he possessed with the result that his characteristic indolence has deepened into a pervasive malaise and his habitual fears have turned into "terrours." Things have gotten worse and Johnson seems helpless in the face of this downturning. He depicts himself as "the bruised reed" and for the first time his customary tone of heroic resolve starts to give way to self-pity. All he can do is to describe what he feels; there is no attempt to account for its existence, either here or in any of the later meditations.

Reflection on his spiritual state, normally conducted at Easter, became so painful to Johnson in the ensuing years that there was no such self-examination in either 1762 or 1763. His failure to observe this important ritual is perhaps the best indication that by the spring of 1764 Johnson was clearly entering a period of great psychological stress. All through the Easter weekend of this year, almost as if to make up for those reviews that he had not conducted, Johnson wrote a series of meditations in which he increasingly turned against himself for his failure to amend his life. On Good Friday itself he wrote two separate meditations, in the first of which he rather calmly prays that he may avoid his usual sins—indolence and neglect of divine worship—and be delivered from "vain terrours." (This is the first mention of these terrors since 1761.) But the second meditation, though shorter, reveals that Johnson has much more serious matters in mind than these sins of omission. "I have made no reformation, I have lived totally useless, more sensual in thought and more addicted to wine and meat."[3] His real concern is with his loss of self-discipline and with his subsequent descent into disorder, clearly manifested in the resolve of that day "to put my rooms in order" and to fast.

Johnson felt that he was losing his grip on himself and he was terrified by this fact and its implications. So disturbed was he by what was happening to him that he sat down at 3 A.M. to record the precise nature of his affliction. "My indolence, since my last reception of the Sacrament, has sunk into grosser sluggishness, and my dissipation spread into wilder negligence. My thoughts have been clouded with sensuality, and, except that from the beginning of this year I have in some measure forborn excess of Strong Drink my appetites have predominated over my reason. A kind of strange oblivion has overspread me, so that I know not what has become of the last year." The most obvious point about this passage is that Johnson felt that in almost every important way he had failed to impose appropriate discipline upon himself. Note, in particular, the vivid verbs of this passage—"sunk," "spread," "clouded," and "overspread"—and how they recall the opening lines of *The Vanity of Human Wishes,* where Johnson was also talking about the difficulties inherent in any search for self-mastery. More important, however, than this self-conscious realization was Johnson's unconscious act of self-chastisement. Here we glimpse for almost the first time Johnson turning against himself in anger for his failure to impose greater control upon his life. Frustrated by his inability to subdue his passions, he describes them in the darkest terms possible to impress upon himself their destructive hold. The act of self-examination has been transformed by Johnson into a harrowing trial in which he is both the defendant and the prosecuting attorney. Divided against himself, he has become emotionally paralyzed.

It was almost certainly at this time, that is, in the spring of 1764, that Johnson's old friend from Oxford, Dr. Adams, stopped by to see Johnson in London and found him, as Boswell later recorded, "in a deplorable state, sighing, groaning, talking to himself, and restlessly walking from room to room." Adams, perhaps also eager to preserve his friend's reputation as a man of sense, told Boswell nothing else of this interview except that Johnson was so afflicted by his misery that he remarked "I would consent to have a limb amputated to recover my spirits." On the basis of this meager information Boswell observed simply: "About this time he was afflicted with a very severe return of the hypochondriack disorder, which was ever lurking about him. He was so ill, as, notwithstanding his remarkable love of company, to be entirely averse to society."[4] And there Boswell left the matter, attributing this depression to the constitutional melancholy that he knew Johnson suffered from throughout his life. What Dr. Adams thought was the cause of this problem he never revealed nor did Johnson himself ever say very much about it.

It is almost impossible to trace the history of Johnson's spiritual life for the next two years because the pertinent material is so meager. He continued to record his innermost thoughts in his private journals, all of which dramatize that he had not managed to escape from his self-created wheel of fire. Here is his entry for his birthday, September 18, 1764: "I have now spent fifty five years in resolving, having from the earliest time almost that I can remember been forming schemes of a better life. I have done nothing; the need of doing therefore is pressing, since the time of doing is short."[5] The anger has become darker and more edged, with overtones of despair. The lists of resolves still appear, but more as habit and duty than realistic expressions of intent. Johnson also began to keep a rather detailed diary in January 1765, but by the end of that month he had abandoned it and kept it only intermittently from then on. That year ended on a more serene note and 1766 began better than most of the preceding five years by dint of Johnson's ability to rise early for almost six months. This was a record for Johnson and it gave him great hope that he was emerging from this Slough of Despond. But that hope was dashed in Easter of that year when, conducting his traditional review of the past year, Johnson became obsessed with religious doubts that he tended to describe as scruples.[6] This preoccupation with "scruples," especially when viewed in the context of these Easter prayers as a whole, demonstrates that his "hypochondriack disorder" of 1764 had deepened very critically in the ensuing two years and had raised the specter of doubt and disbelief. And this moment had been so terrifying to Johnson that it had driven him to the edge of madness.

It may well have been at this time, in the spring of 1766, that Johnson confided to the Thrales, whom he had met through Murphy the year before, "the horrible condition of his mind." Mrs. Thrale's account of one such interview, though well known, must be given in full to understand the nature and origin of this depression.

> Mr. Thrale's attentions and my own now became so acceptable to him, that he often lamented to us the horrible condition of his mind, which he said was nearly distracted; and though he charged *us* to make him odd solemn promises of secrecy on so strange a subject, yet when we waited on him one morning, and heard him, in the most pathetic terms, beg the prayers of Dr. Delap, who had left him as we came in, I felt excessively affected

> with grief, and well remember my husband involuntarily lifted up one hand to shut his mouth, from provocation at hearing a man so wildly proclaim what he could at last persuade no one to believe; and what, if true, would have been so very unfit to reveal.[7]

It is now generally agreed, as this passage itself suggests and as later evidence confirms, that the strange subject of this painful confession was Johnson's fear of insanity. This fear, as I have argued earlier, was one of the deepest and most disturbing of Johnson's fears, one that he believed was chronic and that he could never escape from. He had felt its pressure before, especially after he left Oxford as a young man of twenty, and he felt it again now as a middle-aged man of fifty-seven in London. There had been no one moment in which he was sure that he had been mad, but there had been enough small signs in the past few years, especially in 1764, to suggest that what he had always feared might be happening. It was most probably at this time, then, that Johnson purchased a padlock—and perhaps some chains—which he entrusted to Mrs. Thrale with the instruction that if he should become uncontrollable she should lock him up in a private room. And it is now generally accepted that this purchase was motivated not by a masochistic desire to be enchained and beaten by Mrs. Thrale but by a genuine distrust of himself and of the harm that he might cause others. The more sensational interpretation, as W. J. Bate has recently shown, is not borne out by the facts.[8]

We thus have a reasonably clear picture of the emotional collapse that Johnson suffered in his midfifties. But we do not have an entirely satisfactory explanation for this agonizing depression. What caused it? And why did it occur when it did? Neither Boswell nor Mrs. Thrale gives an answer to this question. And Johnson himself said almost nothing.

2

It does seem odd, given what we know of Johnson's life in the 1750s, that he should experience a breakdown of this intensity at this time. He had been, after all, at the height of his intellectual powers, having just emerged from a decade of astounding literary activity and accomplishment during which he had published *The Vanity of Human Wishes,* the periodical essays that had appeared in the *Rambler, Adventurer,* and *Idler,* the *Dictionary,* and *Rasselas.* Thus, as he entered the 1760s, he started to enjoy for the first time in his life public recognition and financial security. George III acknowledged his achievement by granting him a royal pension in 1763 and Trinity College, Dublin, honored him by granting him an honorary degree in 1765. (Oxford would do the same ten years later.) Increasingly recognized as the leading man of letters of his age, Johnson was entering what should have been the happiest decade of his life.

In addition to these public honors, Johnson experienced some private satisfactions that were also important to him. He completed in 1765 his long-delayed edition of Shakespeare; he derived much enjoyment from the newly formed Club, and, above all, he cherished his newest and best friends—Boswell, whom he met in 1763, and the Thrales, to whom he was introduced in 1765. Neither his extraordinary professional achievement nor the richer nature of his personal life, however, mattered as much to Johnson at this time as some pressing psychological and religious concerns.

W. J. Bate has persuasively argued that Johnson's principal concern in the 1760s—and the ultimate but not the sole cause of his breakdown—was with his failure, as he saw it, to meet various expectations that he had set for himself. "As he reached his middle fifties, the wild disparity between his own life, as he saw it, and all that he demanded of himself had increased to such a point . . . that he could feel that the 'madness' he had inherited from old Michael . . . was at last beginning to catch up with him."[9] These expectations centered primarily on how Johnson hoped to conduct his life and on what he hoped to obtain from it. But as the years passed and as Johnson saw what had happened to his own aspirations, his fear of disappointment and his sense of failure came to the fore and threatened to overwhelm him by turning him against himself and against life itself. This view has great force, but it does not give sufficient place to the religious expectations that Johnson had set for himself, that he had struggled to realize, and that he now increasingly felt he could never fulfil.

It is my conviction that the main cause of this breakdown in his mid-fifties was his realization that he had not been able to make his faith the center of his life. Ever since he had read *A*

Serious Call he had struggled to conduct his life according to the letter and the spirit of the Anglican faith. But he had never succeeded in his own mind to realize this ideal; his attempts to do so had always fallen far short of what he considered acceptable. This discrepancy had always been a source of great anguish to Johnson, but it had become expecially painful in recent years, when his customary reviews of his life revealed how little progress he had made in amending it. His lament at Easter 1765 is characteristic of this mood. "I purpose again to partake of the blessed Sacrament, yet when I consider how vainly I have hitherto resolved at this annual commemoration of my Saviour's death to regulate my life by his laws, I am almost afraid to renew my resolutions. Since the last Easter I have reformed no evil habit, my time has been unprofitably spent, and seems as a dream that has left nothing behind. My memory grows confused, and I know not how the days pass over me."[10]

Much of this passage is familiar—the lament for wasted time and for the persistence of bad habits—but much of it is new. Here Johnson expressed for almost the first time his fear that all of his attempts to discipline his life in accord with his religious beliefs had been in vain. Implicit in this admission, moreover, was Johnson's deeper fear that the act of reformation itself, no matter how sincerely desired, was impossible to effect. He had, in short, lost almost all hope that he could ever achieve the moral purity that he deemed necessary for salvation. And it was this concern that preoccupied him most in this period and that he mentioned again and again in his diary.

> Easter 1761: I have resolved, I hope not presumptuously, till I am afraid to resolve again. . . .
> Easter 1764: I am less than commonly oppressed with the sense of sin, and less affected with the shame of idleness. Yet I will not despair. I will pray to God for resolution. . . .
> June 1, 1770: Every man naturally persuades himself that he can keep his resolutions, nor is he convinced of his imbecility but by length of time, and frequency of experiement. . . .
> July 22, 1773: I think I was ashamed or grieved to find how long and how often I had resolved, what yet except for about one half year I have never done . . . whether I have not lived resolving, till the possibility of performance is past, I know not. . . .

> April 14, 1775: When I look back upon resolutions of improvement and amendments . . . when I find that so much of my life has stolen unprofitably away, and that I can descry by retrospection scarcely a few single days properly and vigorously employed, why do I yet try to resolve again?

And this suspicion, that he might never achieve the degree of reformation that he sought, against which he had guarded himself for so long, aroused lingering doubts, and, still worse, plunged him into an immediate depression.

There were two direct consequences of this disturbing suspicion. First, Johnson was forced to reflect once again upon the question of his own spiritual condition. It is not difficult to follow the train of his thought. If he could not amend his life, how could he ever hope to attain that degree of piety that he believed was necessary for his own salvation? And the answer to this question was clear: never. This was the conclusion that Johnson had been struggling against all his life and that he had endeavored to defeat by heroic acts of intellectual and moral discipline. But he *now* realized that these efforts, however well intentioned, were insufficient, that more was still to be done, and that he did not possess the necessary strength to effect the radical reformation of his life that he felt was required. Under the pressure of these fears Johnson's hold on himself and on his faith started to give way and he experienced frightening anxiety. He noted, in particular, in his journal on Easter 1761 that his "terrours and perplexities" had greatly increased. And his journal makes clear that these fears continued to torment him throughout the next six years. Easter 1764: "Deliver me from the distresses of vain terrour and enable me by thy Grace to will and do what may please thee." March 1766: "Relieve my perplexities. Strengthen my resolution, and enable me to do my duty with vigour and constancy.")

Though Johnson himself did not discuss the nature or the origin of these terrors in any of these passages, they have been generally taken as allusions to his fear of insanity. But their immediate context would argue against such a view. Johnson's concern in all of these passages is with his failure to discipline himself religiously so that he can perform those acts that will render the possibility of redemption more certain. There is no evidence that what he fears here is mental disorder; his own comments stress the way in which his passional nature has corrupted his desire for spiritual purity. "My indolence," he observed on April 21, 1764, "has sunk into grosser sluggishness, and my dissipation spread into wilder negligence. My thoughts have been clouded with sensuality." And his fear grew that such a failure of moral discipline would impede, if not preclude, his salvation. This fear had always haunted Johnson but it now became obsessive because he saw that life was so short and death was so near. "The shortness of the time which the common order of nature allows me to expect is very fequently upon my mind. God grant that it may profit me."[11] Under this self-created pressure, Johnson sank into depression and began to question once again the foundation of his faith.

The second important consequence of Johnson's fear that he could not amend his life was that he began to review the nature of his faith only to discover that it was less certain and secure than he wished. Johnson had often conducted such reviews in the past and had always managed to emerge from them with his faith very much intact. But starting in 1760, Johnson began to brood more intensely than ever before on what he called "scruples." He never made clear what he meant by the term, but his own use of it indicates that he thought of the term in two distinct ways, both of which were sanctioned by the definition he gave in the *Dictionary:* "doubt, difficulty of determination; perplexity generally about minute things." Johnson thought of scruple as doubt, especially religious doubts or concerns, as in the phrase "vain scruples," but he also used the word to indicate perplexity about a relatively minor thing such as his enigmatic note of 1783, "to endeavour to conquer scruples, about Comedy."[12] It is almost certain that Johnson had the former notion in mind when he began to reflect seriously on this subject in the 1760s. A quotation from Jeremy Taylor under "scruple" in the *Dictionary* gives a more precise sense of what the word meant to Johnson than his own vague usage: "For the matter of your confession, let it be secure and serious; but yet so as it may be without any inordinate anxiety, and unnecessary scruples, which only entangle the soul." Scruples meant to Johnson, then, all the disturbing doubts that a Christian might have about the conduct of his religious life as well as about the certainty of his faith. Such doubts were to an extent commonplace but they were also to be quickly overcome.

The first substantial reference to this subject occurs in an undated meditation entitled "Scruples," which Johnson transcribed in 1768 but which probably was written earlier. The most recent editors of this passage tentatively place it in 1759 but this seems too early.[13] A more probable date is 1765 or 1766, when Johnson himself was profoundly preoccupied with these matters. Prior to 1766, there are only two references—in 1757 and in 1764—but during 1766, and especially at Easter, Johnson was deeply troubled by scruples. He began the year by resolving on New Year's Day "to combat scruples" and then on Good Friday he noted that "Scruples distract me, but at Church I had hopes to conquer them." Uncharacteristically, he had failed to record with his usual care the approach of Easter this year and thus felt he had much ground to make up if he were to observe it with the full reverence that he felt was proper. The scruples that he felt now undoubtedly related to this failure of religious duty, but more serious concerns kept pressing upon mind. "I had this day," he wrote the day before Easter, "a doubt like Baxter of my State, and found that my faith though weak, was yet Faith. O God strengthen it." But he is unable to repress further thoughts about scruples, mentioning them again as a cause of worry—"they still distress me"—and placing them first on his list of resolutions. And he then concludes this long rambling entry with a very moving but highly rhetorical prayer that in spite of its controlled power cannot conceal the extent of Johnson's anxiety. "O God, grant me repentance, grant me reformation. Grant that I may be no longer disturbed with doubts and harrassed with vain terrours. Grant that I may no more linger in perplexity, nor waste in idleness that life which thou hast given and preserved. Grant that I may serve thee with firm faith and diligent endeavour, and that I may discharge the duties of my calling with tranquility and constancy."[14]

From this evidence, it is not difficult to discern the origin of Johnson's distress. He had come as close as he ever came to rejecting the faith upon which he had based his life. As the prayer quoted above reveals, Johnson was disturbed by doubts that had caused him to question the grounds on which he had based his faith. This is in fact one of the rare places in the diaries where the word "doubts" appears, having somehow survived the sharp-eyed scrutiny of George Strahan, the early editor, who went to great lengths to cross out any references that would impugn Johnson's reputation for piety. Johnson himself revealed neither here nor elsewhere the exact circumstances that precipitated this spiritual crisis but his reference to his own depressed state—to his doubts, terrors, and perplexities—makes it almost certain that his own wretched condition had caused him to reflect more profoundly than ever before on human suffering and on the essential misery of human life. And this reflection had inevitably led him to take up the whole problem of evil and to question the providential ordering of the universe. Johnson had always resisted such moments of religious reflection in the past by seeking solace in the traditional explanations and by engaging in more intense acts of religious devotion. On this occasion, however, such measures were inadequate, largely because he had gone to the heart of the matter. Why does man suffer in a world governed by God? Finding no satisfactory answer and shaken by his own apparent lack of faith, Johnson did what he so often did on such occasions, he turned to someone whom he had read in the past and who he recalled had suffered from much the same kind of spiritual agony that he was now undergoing.

3

He turned to Richard Baxter, the great Puritan churchman whom Johnson praised to Boswell on several occasions and whom James Gray has argued Johnson respected most of the dissenting divines of the seventeenth century.[15] Johnson does not make clear which work of Baxter he picked up, but from the general context of this remark it would seem plausible that he turned to the two chapters of Baxter's autobiography, *Reliquiae Baxterianae,* in which Baxter discusses the history of his own spiritual life. Johnson might well have remembered this section from an earlier reading since it spoke so directly to his own condition. And he was not, as he tells us, disappointed. What was there, in particular, that proved reassuring to Johnson?

There was, first of all, the fundamental structure of the analysis in which Baxter compared his youthful with his mature beliefs. By engaging in such a spiritual review Baxter directly sanctioned the kind of self-examination that Johnson was himself conducting as well as reinforced Johnson's conviction that such reviews were indispensable to spiritual progress.

Second, Baxter made clear that as he had grown older he had

become less preoccupied with doctrinal disputes and much more concerned with the central articles of faith. "In my youth I was quickly past my fundamentals and was running up into a multitude of controversies. . . . But the elder I grew the smaller stress I laid upon these controversies and curiosities. . . . And now it is the fundamental doctrines of the Catechism which I highliest value and daily think of, and find most useful to myself and others."[16] Johnson, of course, had never participated in the kind of ecclesiastical controversies Baxter had in mind, nor had he ever put much stock in the doctrinal differences that divided one Christian sect from another. He was, as Chester Chapin has shown, remarkably ecumenical in spirit and he always cared far more about his own religious condition than he did about a theological quarrel.[17] Johnson would have agreed heartily with Baxter's concluding remarks on this subject. "In a word, my meditations must be most upon the matters of my practice and interest. And as the love of God and the seeking of everlasting life is the matter of my practice and my interest, so must it be of my meditation. That is the best doctrine and study which maketh men better and tendeth to make them happy."

Third, and much closer to Johnson's own personal concerns at this time, was Baxter's admission that when he was younger "I never was tempted to doubt the truth of Scripture or Christianity, but all my doubts and fears were exercised at home about my own sincerity and interest in Christ . . . since then my sorest assaults have been on the other side, and such they were that, had I been void of internal experience and the adhesion of love, and the special help of God . . . I had certainly apostasized to infidelity." No statement could have described more accurately the quandary in which Johnson found himself at the moment. He, too, had not seriously questioned the truth of his faith since he had been a young man, and he too was now doing so with an intensity that frightened him. What he did not possess as fully as Baxter was a sense of "the special help of God," and it was on this point that Johnson sought most reassurance. Baxter could not provide such assurance, but he offered something that was almost more precious to Johnson. He encouraged Johnson not to feel guilty if he entertained such doubts and to regard them as an integral and inescapable part of man's uncertain condition. "There is many a one," reassured Baxter, "that hideth his temptations to infidelity because he thinketh it a shame to open them, and because it may generate doubts in others; but I doubt the imperfection of most men's care of their salvation . . . doth come from the imperfection of their belief of Christianity and of the life to come." What Baxter implies here he makes explicit later on, namely, the uncertainty that is inherent in any human attempt to ground faith in reason. And it is at this point that Baxter confesses what I think Johnson considered "Baxter's scruple."

What was important to Johnson was both what Baxter said and the undefensive way in which he said it. "Among truths certain in themselves," Baxter wrote, "all are not equally certain unto me; and even of the mysteries of the Gospel I must needs say with Mr. Richard Hooker that whatever men may pretend, the subjective certainty cannot go beyond the objective evidence." Baxter's point was simple, familiar, and orthodox, but it helped Johnson to regain perspective on this timeless problem. It is worthwhile, in spite of its length, to quote in full the passage in which Baxter builds a pyramid of certainty that undoubtedly would have appealed to Johnson's empirical mind.

> Therefore I do more of late than ever discern a necessity of a methodical procedure in maintaining the doctrine of Christianity, and of beginning at natural verities. . . . And it is a marvelous great help to my faith to find it built on so sure foundations and so consonant to the law of nature. I am not so foolish as to pretend my certainty to be greater than it is merely because it is a dishonour to be less certain, nor will I by shame be kept from confessing those infirmities which those have as much as I who hypocritically reproach me with them. My certainty that I am a man before my certainty that there is a God . . . my certainty that there is a God is greater than my certainty that he requireth love and holiness of his creature: my certainty of this is greater than my certainty of the life of reward and punishment hereafter; my certainty of that is greater than my certainty of the endless duration of it and of the immortality of individuate souls . . . my certainty of the Christian faith in its essentials is greater than my certainty of the perfection . . . of all the Holy Scriptures. . . . So that as you see by what gradations my understanding doth proceed, so also that my certainty differs as the evidences differ.

By such reasoning as this, Johnson discovered that his faith, though weak, was faith. And in that simple assertion is Johnson's most explicit admission that he had passed through this dark night of the soul and that he had not yielded to the skepticism that he feared. He had rather reaffirmed his faith, perhaps much as Baxter had in the passage quoted above, and had regained his conviction that life meant most when conducted in the spirit of Christian truths. This reaffirmation, this recovery, was not instantaneous or complete; it took place gradually over the next two years and it involved many terrible moments in which Johnson once again was "disturbed and unsettled for a long time" by vain terrors and fears. On August 17, 1767, Johnson noted he "obtained sudden and great relief, and had freedom of mind restored to me, which I have wanted for all this year without being able to find any means of obtaining it.[18] But on September 18, 1769, Johnson wrote that the preceding year, 1768, "has been wholly spent in a slow progress of recovery."[19] The second great crisis of Johnson's life was over. There were still bad moments when he turned upon himself for his failure to amend his life. But the worst was over; and his faith, though weak, was still faith.

4

There should be now no doubt that it was Johnson's need to believe that enabled him to regain his faith. His reading in Baxter had made him realize that "subjective certainty cannot go beyond objective evidences," and since proof in such matters was impossible, he could only possess faith if he were willing to surrender his demand for rational proof and accept something less certain. Baxter had helped Johnson to make this choice; but it must also be said that Johnson *wanted* to make the same choice. He did not want to abandon the faith in which he had been raised and by which he had conducted his life. To have done so would have rendered him helpless and terrified; it would have left him without direction and without purpose. He had the courage to question his faith; he had the courage, almost in spite of himself, to confront the specter of skepticism; but he did not have the courage to abandon his faith. He needed his faith to control and combat his fears. And I suspect that it was this conviction that impelled him to jot down in his diary for August 9, 1777, "Faith in some proportion to

Fear."[20] He meant that his faith must be at least as strong as his fears if he were to maintain his emotional well-being. So far his faith had possessed such strength, but could he sustain such faith as he neared the end of his journey?

7

The Last Great Trial

Those who have endeavoured to teach us to die well, have taught few to die willingly; yet I cannot but hope that a good life might end at last in a contented death.
Johnson to Joseph Baretti

Johnson's whole life, as Sir John Hawkins shrewdly noted, "was a preparaton for his death."[1] So much of what he had said and done had been undertaken in anticipation of this final moment. Uncertain of when death would come, he had driven himself mercilessly to prepare himself for it and for the act of divine judgment that he believed would follow. And thus, when on June 16, 1783, he suffered a terrible stroke, in which he was temporarily deprived of speech, he realized that "the end of the journey" was near. Although Johnson had asserted on an earlier occasion that "it matters not how a man dies, but how he lives," and that "the act of dying is not of importance, it lasts so short a time," nevertheless now that his own life was drawing to a close Johnson clung to what remained with extraordinary tenacity and did everything in his power to insure that he would receive divine grace.[2] He knew it would "do no good to whine," but he also knew that he could not submit to his fate without doing all that he thought was right. He was approaching "the last great trial" of his soul in its struggle to achieve salvation. He was at the same time submitting his own faith to its greatest test. The night had almost come when he could no longer work. Would his faith sustain him through this dark hour or would it give way under the pressure of what Johnson had years before called "the horrour of the last"?

2

In the last year and a half before his death, Johnson conducted himself in much the same way that he had in the rest of his life. He said little about himself, recorded but did not dwell on the state of his health, continued to read and write, maintained an active social life, and made numerous short visits to old friends and relations. As Boswell observed, Johnson "did not hide his head from the world, in solitary abstraction; he did not deny himself to the visits of his friends and acquaintances; but at all times, when he was not overcome by sleep, was ready for conversation as in his best days."[3] Perhaps the best evidence of Johnson's extraordinary vitality at this time was the enormous number of letters that he wrote, which as a whole exhibit, as Boswell noted, "a genuine and noble specimen of vigour and vivacity of mind, which neither age nor sickness could impair or diminish."[4] The vitality of his spirit was indisputable, but it could not prevent the eventual return of those doubts and fears that had haunted Johnson for so long. He was as reticent as he had ever been about these distressing matters and as reluctant to record them in his diaries as he was to discuss them in public discourse. The repression that he had habitually practiced in this realm of experience was more intense than ever before. The stern advice that he had testily given to Boswell, who had complained of his melancholy a few years before, Johnson now directed at himself. "No man talks of that which he is desirous to conceal, and every man desires to conceal that of which he is ashamed. Do not pretend to deny it; *manifestum habemus furem;* make it an invariable and obligatory law to yourself, never to mention your own mental diseases. If you are never to speak of them you will think on them but little, and if you think little of them, they will molest you rarely . . . therefore, from this hour speak no more, think no more about them."[5] The point was well taken but finally irrelevant; for Johnson's apprehensions, to return to Boswell's famous metaphor, "like the wild beasts of the Arena were still around him and, despite conflict and repression, were still assailing him."

Of these apprehensions, the worst by far was still his fear of death, which he continually sought to repress but which expressed itself more and more as his habitual control gave way under the pressure of increased concern. Writing to Boswell in February 1784, Johnson concluded a report of his health with a poignant remark: "I am extremely afraid of dying."[6] The old fear had not disappeared nor had it been substantially alleviated by religious consolation; it existed more than ever as an inescapable reality. His own condition, and that of many of his friends, had made that clear to him. "On which side soever I turn," he wrote Reynolds in August 1784, "Mortality presents its formidable frown. I left three old friends at Lichfield, when I was last there, and now found them all dead. I no sooner lose sight of dear Allen, than I am told that I shall see him no more. That we must all die, we always knew, I wish I had sooner remembered it."[7]

And yet when Mrs. Thrale thoughtlessly urged him to die with dignity, Johnson rejected such advice as pure cant and told her so. "Write to me no more about *dying with a grace.* When you feel what I have felt in approaching Eternity—in fear of soon hearing the sentence of which there is no revocation, you will know the folly, my wish is that you may know it sooner. The distance between the grave and the remotest point of human longevity is but a very little, and of that little no part is certain. You know all this, and I thought that I knew it too, but I know it now with a new conviction."[8] The real reason for this stern rebuke was, of course, that Mrs. Thrale had momentarily forgotten that death for Johnson was always tied up with the problem of salvation. And she had in an unguarded moment touched on the true origin of his fear of death, namely, his horror of not being saved.

In the eight months before he died, this fear became more pronounced than it ever had been before. Determined not "to murmur at the established order of the creation," Johnson took upon himself complete responsibility for his own salvation. He believed that God was just but he still feared the divine verdict because, as he put it, "I cannot be *sure* that I have fulfilled the conditions on which salvation is granted." And since he could not be sure and since he possessed a strong sense of his own sinfulness, he knew that there was a real and frightening possibility that he might be damned. "I am afraid," Johnson informed the amiable but incredulous Dr. Adams, "I may be one of those who shall be damned."[9] Johnson, in spite of all his efforts to discipline himself and to live as a devout Christian, was still not certain that he had done enough to be saved. He did not dare give himself the benefit of the doubt: the risk was too great.

He saw clearly the spiritual limbo in which this uncertainty placed him and he described the dilemma in which he found himself in a very revealing letter that he wrote to Mrs. Thrale in March of this last year:

> You know I never thought confidence with respect to futurity any part of the character of a brave, a wise, or a good man. Bravery has no place where it can avail nothing. Wisdom impresses strongly the consciousness of those faults, of which it is itself perhaps an aggravation; and Goodness always wishing to be better, and imputing every deficience to criminal negligence, and every fault to voluntary corruption, never dares to suppose the conditions of forgiveness fulfilled, nor what is wanting in the crime supplied by Penitence. This is the state of the best, but what must be the condition of him whose heart will not suffer him to rank himself among the best, or among the good, such must be his dread of the approaching trial, as will leave him little attention to the opinion of those whom he is leaving for ever, and the serenity that is not felt, it can be no virtue to feign.[10]

Johnson had never thought of himself as "among the best," nor did he think so now.

Johnson's refusal to give himself the benefit of the doubt arose from his continuing conviction of his own sinfulness and his inability to dispel the perplexities that had always troubled him. He referred to these fears in one way or another in every prayer that he wrote during this year with the single exception, significantly, of the last. Here are some excerpts from the most notable examples.

> January 1. I beseech thee . . . [to] give me such ease of body as may enable me to be useful, and remove from me all such scruples and perplexities as encumber and obstruct my mind. . . .
> April 11 (Easter). Let my purposes be good and my resolutions unshaken, and let me not be hindred or disturbed by vain and useless fears. . . .
> August 1. Assist me in this commemoration by thy Holy Spirit that I may look back upon the sinfulness of my life past with pious sorrow, and efficacious Repentance . . . that I may be freed from vain and useless scruples.

These excerpts make clear what his longer prayer, "Against Inquisitive and Perplexing Thoughts," confirms, namely, that there were two main sources of anxiety.[11] The first pertained to what Johnson called scruples, by which he meant all those doubts that continually haunted him regarding his religious conduct. These concerns ranged, as I have earlier noted, from his failure to observe various devotional practices to his fear that he had not sufficiently amended his life. And Johnson was naturally very anxious at this late time to establish once and for all the genuineness of his piety and the sincerity of his desire for repentance. It is this issue that Johnson had in mind when he wrote in the opening of his prayer: "O Lord, my Maker and Protector, who hast graciously sent me into this world, to work out my salvation, enable me to drive from me all such unquiet and perplexing thoughts as may mislead or hinder me in the practice of those duties which thou has required."

The second source of discomfort arose mainly from his skeptical cast of mind, which acknowledged the limitations of human knowledge, recognized that "Thy thoughts are not my thoughts," but was always receptive to possible new evidence about the spiritual world. This receptiveness made Johnson willing to believe the story of the apparition of a woman who accurately predicted the time of Lord Lyttelton's death and to reject Dr. Adams's claim that he had enough evidence for the existence of the spiritual world without relying on such extraordinary episodes.[12] While Johnson realized that excessive preoccupation with such insoluble problems might well lead to skepticism, nevertheless such speculation could not be suppressed, though it needed to be controlled. Hence his plea in the same prayer that the Holy Spirit "would withdraw [his] Mind from unprofitable and dangerous enquiries, from difficulties vainly curious, and doubts impossible to be solved." The extent of Johnson's concern with this critical problem is further evidenced by the notes he left in his journal—under October 31—apparently for an essay on the causes of skepticism.

SKEPTICISM CAUSED BY

1. Indifference about opinions.
2. Supposition that things disputed are disputable.
3. Denial of unsuitable evidence.
4. False judgement of Evidence.

5. Complaint of the obscurity of Scripture.
6. Contempt of Fathers and of authority.
7. Absurd method of learning objection first.
8. Study not for truth but vanity.

Ep to Gal written against the Hebionites
Desposyni q. Montagu. 232.

---

9. Sensuality and a vicious life.
10. False honour, false shame.
11. Omission of prayer and religious Exercises.[13]

We do not know for certain why Johnson was considering such an essay. It may have been related to his intention to compose a book of prayers; it may just as well have been related to his desire to test the strength of his own belief for one last time. This was the kind of test that appealed to Johnson and he passed it easily. He had thought the matter out; he had discovered its causes; and he might well have written about it had he felt more urgency or enjoyed better health.

As real and as powerful as these fears were, they proved unable to undercut the substance of Johnson's faith. They continued to trouble him until the very end, but they were never able to drive him onto the shoals of skepticism or into the abyss of atheism. For the most important fact of the last nine months of Johnson's life was that he underwent a quasi-mystical experience that brought him substantial relief from the spiritual anxiety that he had almost always known. Here for the first time Johnson thought that his actions had been deemed acceptable. Here for the first time Johnson dared to believe that he had been saved.

3

The initial phase of this important spiritual transformation occurred toward the end of February 1784. In the preceding December, Johnson had suffered a serious asthmatic attack, which had confined him to his house and which had depressed his spirits. "I may be allowed to be weary of telling that I am sick, and sick," he wrote Queeney Thrale on January 31, "and you may well be weary of hearing, but having now kept the house for seven weeks, and not being likely soon to come out, I have my want of health much in my mind, and am indeed very deeply dejected."[14] Johnson was eventually confined for 129 days, that is, from December 1783 until April 1784. To make matters worse, Johnson was afflicted in early February with a very dangerous dropsy, which he feared he would not be able to control.

The combination of the asthma and the dropsy made him realize that his death could not be far off. He told Sir John Hawkins, "with a look that cut me to the heart . . . that he had the prospect of death before him, and that he dreaded to meet his Saviour." Hawkins tried to console him by reminding Johnson of "the services he had rendered to the cause of religion and virtue, as well as by his example, as his writings," but he would not be easily solaced. "Every man," retorted Johnson with characteristic candor, "knows his own sins, and also, what grace he has resisted. But, to those of others, and the circumstances under which they were committed, he is a stranger: he is, therefore, to look on himself as the greatest sinner that he knows of." The argument and the tone are familiar; it is what Johnson said to others—and indeed to himself—on counteless occasions. But there is now a note of urgency, a sense that the end that he had always dreaded was very near. The full force of this realization impelled him to see his plight with poignant clarity. At the end of this dialogue with Hawkins, Johnson turned to his friend and asked: "Shall I, who have been a teacher of others, myself be a castaway?" Hawkins, aware that the question was in fact self-directed, gave no answer.[15]

Johnson then pursued the only course open to him, that of more fervent piety. "He declared," as Hawkins later noted, "his intention to employ the whole of the next day in fasting, humiliation, and such other devotional exercises, as became a man in his situation." He shut himself alone in his room, told Francis Barber to admit no one "for your master is preparing himself to die," and devoted the entire day to religious reflection and purification. When Hawkins came to visit the following day, Johnson described how "in the course of this exercise, he found himself relieved from that disorder which had been growing on him . . . by a gradual evacuation of water to the amount of twenty pints, a like instance whereof he had never before experienced, and asked [Hawkins] what [he] thought of it." Hawkins explained that he thought "God had wrought a miracle . . . and that he had not in vain humbled himself before his Maker." And Hawkins then recorded that Johnson "seemed to acquiesce in all that I said on this important subject, and several times, cried out, 'It is wonderful, very wonderful.'"[16]

Hawkins's account is the only firsthand report preserved of this important moment. Johnson made no mention of it in his own journals, but he did write Lucy Porter about it just two days after it happened. "I have been extremely ill of an Asthma and dropsy, but received by the mercy of God sudden and unexpected relief last thursday by the discharge of twenty pints of water."[17] He described this same event to Boswell when he came to London in May. On the basis of these references it is clear that Johnson, though reluctant to attribute his relief to divine intervention, believed that God had extended his mercy and granted him a miraculous reprieve. Johnson did not change his mind on this matter later, even though he discovered that Dr. Heberden had known four other examples of such sudden relief. Johnson, when he came to tell Boswell of the experience, was still reluctant to ascribe the change to an act of divine mercy but, as Boswell noted, "from his manner of telling it, I could perceive that it appeared to him as something more than an incident in the common course of events."[18]

It is clear from the tone of Boswell's remark that Johnson thought he had been the recipient of divine grace. But owing to his fear of spiritual pride he was reluctant to admit to himself that he had been saved. As he remarked to Boswell a week after his original account of the experience, "some people are not afraid [of death], because they look upon salvation as the effect of an absolute decree, and think they feel in themselves the marks of sancitfication. Others, and those the most rational in my opinion, look upon salvation as conditional; and as they never can be sure that they have complied with the conditions, they are afraid."[19] What Johnson wished to affirm was that his love of virtue and his reverence for religion had at last been acknowledged. He wanted to believe that all his endeavors to make his faith the center of his moral being had finally and mercifully been accepted.

The fullest expression he gave of this hope occurred just two weeks before he died, but it had clearly been on his mind since the beginning of the year. "I had, very early in my life, the seeds of goodness in me: I had a love of virtue, and a reverence for religion; and these, I trust, have brought forth in me fruits meet for repentance; and, if I have repented as I ought, I am forgiven. I have, at times, entertained a loathing of sin and of myself, particularly at the beginning of this year, when I had the prospect of death before me; and this has not abated when my fears of death have been less; and, at these times, I have had such rays of hope shot into my soul, as have almost persuaded me, that I am in a state of reconciliation with God.[20] As hesitant as Johnson was to believe that his "wonderful" experience was a mark of sanctification, he clearly now saw it as a sign that he would be saved at the last.[21]

4

This "wonderful" experience brought new hope to Johnson, which was all the more remarkable because it occurred against a backdrop of increasingly failing health and depressed spirits. Although he recovered enough in the spring to permit him to resume his social life and to encourage him to take one last journey to visit his old friends, he knew that this relief was temporary. But far worse than even this realization was his increased sense of loneliness. So many of his old friends had already died—Henry Thrale in 1781; Robert Levet in 1782; Anna Williams in 1783—and so many others who still lived were busy with their own affairs. Boswell, aside from his visit in the spring, was now almost totally absorbed by his legal career in Edinburgh, while Mrs. Thrale had retreated to Bath, where, still unbeknownst to Johnson, she was contemplating her marriage to Piozzi. With the death of Levet and Williams, Johnson's own turbulent household had largely dissolved, leaving him only with Francis Barber, and perhaps Mrs. Desmoulins, to relieve his solitude. And after the painful break with Mrs. Thrale in July, Johnson lost forever "the dearest of dear ladies." What he wrote to Mrs. Thrale almost a year before applied now more than ever. Johnson had then remarked: "I am now broken with disease, without the alleviation of familiar friendship, or domestick society; I have no middle state between clamour and silence, between general conversation and self-tormenting solitude."[22] It was against this background of disease and depression, of loss and loneliness, that Johnson's faith asserted itself and increasingly granted him a peace of mind that he had rarely known. This was the most significant general effect that his February experience had upon him; and it manifested itself by a dramatic intensification of his devotional piety.

Johnson had argued long ago in *Rambler* 69 that "piety [was] the only proper and adequate relief of decaying man" and that religious hope was absolutely necessary to bear the inevitable spiritual anxiety of the last: "He that grows old without religious hopes, as he declines into imbecility, and feels pains and sorrows incessantly crowding upon him, falls into a gulph of bottomless misery, in which every reflection must plunge him deeper, and where he finds only new gradations of anguish, and precipices of horrour." And Johnson now turned with great fervor to this self-created prescription for spiritual health to enable him to get through the little time that was left.

The act of prayer continued to be the most important and satisfying expression of his piety. The prayers of this last year are remarkably similar to those of the past in tone and in substance. Johnson continued to the end to berate himself for his own unworthiness and for his failure to amend his life. He continued to ask forgiveness, to seek repentance, and to purify himself. But a significant new note is struck. There is a genuine ring of joy in Johnson's voice, expressing profound gratitude for the deliverance from death, for the additional time he had been granted to work out his salvation, and for the grace that he felt had been extended to him in his "wonderful" experience. His prayer of September 5, written while he was visiting John Taylor at Ashbourne, exemplifies this new tone. "Almighty Lord and merciful Father, to Thee be thanks, and praise for all thy mercies, for the awakening of my mind, the continuance of my life, the amendment of my health, and the opportunity now granted of commemorating the death of thy Son Jesus Christ, our mediator and Redeemer.[23]

Another manifestation of this increased piety, which may have ultimately derived from his miraculous experience, was his willingness to consider the compilation of an anthology of prayers, including some of his own, to which he would add a "discourse on prayer." Johnson had thought about such a book for a number of years but had always put it off; he mentioned it again in June of this year to Dr. Adams and Boswell, both of whom urged him to execute his plan. Johnson, however, suddenly recoiled, as Boswell noted, "at the manner of our importunity, and in great agitation called out, 'Do not talk thus of what is so aweful. I know not what time God will allow me in this world. There are many things which I wish to do.' Some of us persisted, and Dr. Adams said, 'I never was more serious about anything in my life.' Johnson. 'Let me alone, let me alone; I am overpowered.' And then he put his hands before his face, and reclined for some time upon the table."[24]

Johnson never completed this project, though he did get so far as to jot down some notes toward it, labeled "Preces," in his journal. These notes are rather puzzling; for there is no discernible logic in them, except that most of them have clearly been inspired by his own preoccupation with disease, the death of his friends, and his own approaching death. Far more important, however, than Johnson's failure to complete this project was his reaction to the pressure that his well-intentioned friends had placed upon him. Why was he overpowered by their exhortation? It was not, of course, the nature of the undertaking that upset him; for this was the kind of project that appealed to him and that he could perform easily, having studied the subject all of his life. It was rather that this proposal reminded him of all the things that he had meant to do but had somehow left undone. It reminded him, in particular, of so many of his religious resolutions, which he had formed again and again but which had so often gone unpracticed. It reminded him, above all, of how much he had failed to do and how little time he now had left in which to do it.

Of equal importance with prayer as a manifestation of Johnson's deepening piety was his stricter observance of Holy Communion. Although Johnson had always intended to take this sacrament as often as he could, his practice was erratic and was confined mainly to Easter. In this last year, however, Johnson took Holy Communion on April 11, August 1, September 5, and then for the last time on December 5. More important still was the fact that the ceremony itself was mentioned with much greater frequency and with much greater meaning than it had been in the past. The sacrament of the Eucharist that Johnson had once treated very much as a religious obligation had taken on new and greater significance. Never before had he thanked God, as he had in the prayer quoted above, for the opportunity to celebrate the death of Christ. Never before had he alluded so often to Christ as "our mediator and Redeemer."

Johnson had in fact developed a new attitude toward the

figure of Christ and the meaning of Christ's death. For most of his own life, Johnson had thought of Christ as a largely symbolic figure, whose life served as the ultimate model for the aspiring Christian and whose death saved man from the inexorable demands of divine justice. On the whole, Christ's life never mattered as much as his death to Johnson. There is almost no mention of any of the main events of his life nor any discussion of his teachings. Most of Johnson's references to Christ were impersonal and confined to the ritualized endings of his prayers. When Johnson did speak of Christ, it was almost always in connection with doctrinal matters, his place in the Trinity, or his significance in the Eucharist. And even in these instances, there was something detached about Johnson's attitude toward Christ. He saw him not as a real person or as a powerful presence, but rather as a part of a plan of divine justice. And this same attitude manifested itself in his attitude toward Christ's death. God made Christ an example to mankind of how sin would be punished in the world. Christ became the principal means by which God satisfied his need for divine justice and thus established his moral government of the universe.

Recent scholarship, however, has convincingly demonstrated that Johnson's attitude toward the death of Christ underwent a significant change in the last eleven years of his life. In 1773, in conversation with Boswell, Johnson had expressed an essentially "exemplary" view of the Crucifixion in which he argued that it satisfied the need for divine justice and that it acted as a deterrent to sin. "He said his notion was, that it [Christ's death] did not atone for the sins of the world; but, by satisfying divine justice, by shewing that no less than the Son of God suffered for sin, it shewed to men and innumerable created beings, the heinousness of it, and therefore rendered it unnecessary for divine vengeance to be exercised against sinners, as it otherwise must have been; that in this way . . . the effect it should produce would be repentance and piety, by impressing upon the mind a just notion of sin."[25] This view, which Johnson had held for all of his adult life, most probably derived, as Maurice Quinlan has shown, from Law.[26] It was not an uncommon view and had been widely held in the preceding century.

In 1781, just eight years later, Johnson had adopted an essentially different view of the atonement in which he now stressed the "expiatory" character of the act. He did not reject out of hand, however, his earlier conviction in the enactment of divine justice or in the need for God to dramatize his hatred of sin. As Johnson made clear to Boswell, the death of Christ was still to "be considered as necessary to the government of the universe, that God should make known his perpetual and irreconcileable detestation of moral evil." But Johnson now believed that "when justice is appeased, there is a proper place for the exercise of mercy; and that such propitiation shall supply, in some degree, the imperfections of our obedience, and the inefficacy of our repentance: for, obedience and repentance, such as we can perform, are still necessary." What he had once denied he now accepted as possible: Christ's death had at least *partially* atoned for man's sins. His death was not just a dramatic example of God's "detestation of moral evil" but more importantly a moving testimony to God's concern for man. God sought not revenge but repentance and reformation. "As the end of punishment is not revenge of crimes, but propagation of virtue, it was more becoming the Divine clemency to find another manner of proceeding, less destructive to man, and at least equally powerful to promote goodness." And the means to that end was the sacrifice of Christ's life for the sins of mankind. "The peculiar doctrine of Christianity is," as Johnson remarked in a paragraph that he added to his original statement, "that of an universal sacrifice and perpetual propitiation."[27] It is important to clarify here that Johnson did not mean to imply by "perpetual propitiation" the notion that man had been completely and forever forgiven of his sins. He meant rather that Christ's sacrifice had won for all men the chance to regain God's grace and to achieve salvation, *if* man continued to seek obedience and repentance. Christ's act had not absolved man of all moral responsibility; it merely gave man the opportunity to exert such responsibility. Christ's death had created the possibility of redemption; it fell to man to make it come true.

The precise reason for this profound change is not clear. It may well have been caused, as Maurice Quinlan has shrewdly suggested, by an intense religious experience Johnson underwent at Easter 1776 and by his reading of Samuel Clarke's sermons.[28] It may also have been brought about by his close study of the Bible, which he read in its entirety for the first time in 1772 and which he now read more steadily than at any earlier point in his life. He studied, in particular, the New Testament either in Greek or in some English translation. Whatever the cause, the effect was clear. Johnson had a much more personal attitude toward Christ and a much more passionate conviction of him as the Redeemer. It is almost as if Johnson felt for the first time that Christ was a real man who had given his own life so that mankind could be saved. In the prayers of 1781, Johnson expressed much more feeling for the sacrament of Holy Communion than he ever had before and even resolved at one point to take "the Sacrament at least three times a year."[29] "By this awful Festival," he wrote on Easter Eve, "is particularly recommended Newness of Life, and a new Life I will now endeavour to begin by more diligent application to useful employment, and more frequent attendance on publick worship."[30] And as poems of these last years, such as "Christ to the Sinner," reveal, it is the person of Christ who now most interests Johnson. It is Christ who gives solace, joy, and comfort to sinful man.

And thus the most conspicuous feature of Johnson's religious life in the nine months before his death was his deeper faith in the possibility of enjoying "a happy futurity." He had argued over thirty years before in *Rambler* 203 for the importance of such belief in order "to cheer the gloom of the last hour." He wrote then: "But futurity has still its prospects; there is yet happiness in reserve, which, if we transfer our attention to it, will support us in the pains of disease, and the languor of decay. This happiness we may expect with confidence, because it is out of the power of chance, and may be attained by all that sincerely desire and earnestly pursue it. On this therefore every mind ought finally to rest. Hope is the chief blessing of man, and that hope only is rational, of which we are certain that it cannot deceive us." As a result of his "wonderful" experience Johnson now possessed such hope. Although he was still pained by reflection upon his past, nevertheless he was no longer as deeply troubled by the uncertainty of the future. Writing to John Ryland on September 2, Johnson observed: "From the retrospect of life when solitude, leisure, accident, or darkness turn my thoughts upon it, I shrink with multiplicty of horrour. I look forward with less pain. Behind, is wickedness and folly, before, is the hope of repentance, the possibility of amendment, and the final hope of everlasting mercy.[31] No longer does he berate himself for what he has not done; no longer does he chide himself for having failed to reform his conduct. He emphasizes instead what he can still do; he stresses instead his hope of self-improvement and divine mercy. He no longer distrusts such hopes; on the contrary he sees them as the only true source of solace. This conviction grew stronger with each passing month until Johnson was finally able to confess to a spiritual serenity that he had never known before. "My mind," he wrote John Ryland on October 6, "is calmer than in the beginning of the year, and I comfort myself with hopes of every kind, niether despairing of ease in this world, nor of happiness in another."[32] Such was the mellow state of mind that Johnson had reached in the late fall.

5

The third and final stage of Johnson's spiritual progress occurred during the last month of his life, from his return to London from the Midlands on November 16 until his death at home on December 13. During this time the asthma and the dropsy with which he had been afflicted for so long and from which he had enjoyed a reprieve over the summer now grew worse by the day. And to these afflictions was added a very painful inflammation of the testicle, which his doctors were naturally reluctant to puncture. Above all, the medications provided little or no relief and, in the case of opium, made matters worse. Johnson knew that death was very near and made no real efforts to fight what he now accepted as inevitable. He even stopped recording the state of his health in his journal on November 8. What little time there was should clearly be spent in arranging his affairs and in performing appropriate religious devotions.

Johnson went to extraordinary lengths to make sure that he had done all those things that he ought to have done. He thus ordered gravestones and wrote epitaphs for his parents and brother; he sent Pembroke College a gift of his collected works; he gave George Strahan his prayers and meditations for publication; he burned a mass of his most personal papers; and at last, after much prodding from Sir John Hawkins, he made his will. Busy as he was attending to these affairs, Johnson was most deeply concerned with the religious preparations for his death. He engaged in daily private prayer, usually with his servant Francis Barber, and he took Holy Communion as often as he could, usually at home, receiving it for the last time on Sunday, December 5, eight days before he died. He continued to find particular satisfaction and solace in Clarke's *Sermons* and in the New Testament. And he continued to discuss religious questions until the very end. He gave to William Windham the fullest and most precise defense he ever made for belief in revealed religion as well as his final affirmation in the expiatory character of Christ's death.[34] He exhorted all of his friends whom he saw at this time "to attend closely to every religious duty"; and he particularly "enforced the obligation of private prayer and receiving the Sacrament."[34] But what was Johnson's true state of mind as he neared his end?

Hawkins provided the best answer to this question when he remarked that "the prospect of the change he [Johnson] was about to undergo, and the thought of meeting his Saviour, troubled him, but . . . he had hope that he would not reject him."[35] Johnson, in short, was still troubled by the fears and doubts that had haunted him throughout his life. He was still torn between his fear of death and his love of life. As Boswell put it, "Death had always been to him an object of terrour; so that, though by no means happy, he still clung to life with an eagerness at which many have wondered."[36] At times he was so overpowered by the thought of his own death that he succumbed to morbidity, but at other times, he was so determined to live that he turned upon those who were closest to him with uncharacteristic anger. When Dr. Brocklesby proved reluctant to puncture Johnson's sarcocele, Johnson exclaimed: "How many men in a year die through the timidity of those whom they consult for health. I want length of life, and you fear giving me pain, which I care not for."[37]

Johnson still did not dare to presume, in spite of his "wonderful" experience, that "the conditions of his forgiveness had been fulfilled, nor what is wanting in the crime supplied by penitence." And as late as Sunday December 5, he was reluctant to accept the traditional argument for solace put forth by John Ryland, who had observed that "we had great hopes given us." To this Johnson replied, "we have hopes given us; but they are conditional, and I know not how far I have fulfilled those conditions."[38] The depth of this uncertainty sustained in Johnson to the end the emotional anguish that led him to recite on occasion Macbeth's poignant query to the doctor regarding his wife's disturbed state: "Canst thou not minister to a mind diseased?" And Johnson acknowledged with characteristic candor the truth of the doctor's response: "Therein the patient must minister unto himself." It should be remembered that at the end of this exchange with Ryland, Johnson added, "I think that I have now corrected all bad and vicious habits." This is a rare and wondrous admission that he may at last have done all that he thought was necessary for his salvation.

Convinced at last that his own efforts, however imperfect, had been accepted, and confident that Christ had died to set man free, Johnson experienced a spiritual serenity that he had not thought possible. He now knew what it meant to be "in a state of reconciliation with God." And the fullest and most transcendent expression of this newfound peace of mind appeared in his last prayer.

> Almighty and most merciful Father, I am now, as to human eyes it seems, about to commemorate for the last time, the death of thy son Jesus Christ, our Saviour and Redeemer. Grant, O Lord, that my whole hope and confidence may be in his merits and in thy mercy: forgive and accept my late conversion, enforce and accept my imperfect repentance; make this commemoration of him available to the confirmation of my Faith, the establishment of my hope, and the enlargment of my Charity, and make the Death of thy son Jesus effectual to my redemption. Have mercy upon me and pardon the multitude of my offenses. Bless my Friends, have mercy upon all men. Support me by the Grace of thy Holy Spirit in the days of weakness, and at the hour of death, and receive me, at my death, to everlasting happiness, for the Sake of Jesus Christ. Amen.[39]

This prayer has been the subject of much unnecessary and senseless misunderstanding, ever since George Strahan copied it from Hawkins and then deleted the clause "forgive and accept my late conversion." We do not know why Strahan removed this clause unless he feared that its presence would somehow impugn Johnson's reputation for piety or call into question Johnson's allegiance to the Anglican church. Somewhat later, to make matters worse, there circulated a rumor that Johnson had experienced a religious conversion of an Evangelical sort shortly before his death. But as Maurice Quinlan pointed out, "there is no clear evidence that Johnson was converted in the Evangelical sense, despite the fact that a rumor to that effect circulated for several decades."[40] More important, however, than this conclusion was Donald Greene's argument that there was no evidence for the belief that the phrase "my late conversion" ever meant to Johnson—or indeed to Strahan and Boswell—a change from the Anglican to the Evangelical faith. There is "no reason for doubting that Johnson meant the word 'conversion' in its classical theological sense, namely as a change from a bad to a holy life." Greene has convincingly demonstrated that to disregard this meaning of the word is "to reduce the whole of Johnson's rich religious life to nonsense."[41] We should thus now look at this prayer not as an expression of new belief but rather as an affirmation of an old dispensation, of a lifelong desire to believe in the truths of Christianity.

The most striking aspect of this prayer, especially given the critical commentary it has inspired, is that Johnson's principal concern is not with his "late conversion" or his "imperfect repentance" but with this last celebration of Holy Communion and this last profession of unqualified faith. His attention is directed not so much at himself, at his own sins and scruples, as it is at Christ as the central figure of the Eucharist and as "our Redeemer and Saviour." His own religious struggle, which had been the principal theme of all the previous prayers, is not even mentioned and is completely ignored in his effort "to make this commemoration of him available to the confirmation of my Faith, the establishment of my hope, and the enlargement of my Charity." He then passes over lightly his "late conversion," taking its existence for granted and attributing no special significance to it.

We cannot know for certain what Johnson meant by this phrase; but it makes most sense to see it in the light of the definition of conversion he gave in the *Dictionary*, as a "change from reprobation to grace, from a bad to a holy life." It might also be helpful to remember a citation from Henry Hammond that Johnson gave under his definition of repentance: "Repentance is a change of mind, or a conversion from sin to God, not some one bare act of change, but a lasting durable state of new life, which is called regeneration." No single statement could describe more accurately what Johnson meant by conversion and what he considered to have happened in his spiritual life in the nine months before his death than this quotation. Johnson had experienced a change of mind or, perhaps more accurately, a deepening of mind in which he became convinced that he had experienced divine grace. He had become convinced, much to his surprise and much beyond his most fervent hopes, that his "wonderful" experience of the previous February had not been "some one bare act of change, but a lasting durable state of new life." The preceding nine months had made the extent of this change clear. And it was Johnson's faith in the meaning of this change that was responsible for the quiet, confident, and serene tone of this last prayer.

Johnson had at last ended his long quest for religious certitude; he had survived his last great trial. What he had achieved at the end was a kind of spiritual integrity, by which I mean not so much honesty, which he always had, as wholeness. He could at last balance his hopes with his fears, his doubts with his convictions, his anxieties with his aspirations. He had at last managed to make his faith the center of his life and to reconcile the discordant parts of his belief into a harmonious whole. Doubt and fear had not been dispelled, but they had been subsumed by his faith. And nowhere did Johnson reveal more clearly and more poignantly the peace of mind that he had at last attained than in the statement he dictated in his last days to Hawkins to be included in his will: "I humbly commit to the infinite and eternal goodness of Almighty God, my soul polluted with many sins; but, as I hope, purified by repentance, and redeemed, as I trust, by the death of Jesus Christ."[43]

Notes

Preface

1. James Boswell, *The Life of Samuel Johnson,* ed. G. B. Hill, rev. and enl. by L. F. Powell, 6 vols., (Oxford: Oxford University Press, 1934–50), 1:67. (Hereafter cited as *Life.*)

2. Samuel Johnson, *The Letters of Samuel Johnson,* ed. R. W. Chapman, 3 vols., (Oxford: Oxford University Press, 1952), no. 970.2. (Hereafter cited as *Letters.*)

3. *Life,* 4:426–27.

4. Isaac Reed, *An Impartial Account of the Life, Character, Genius, and Writings of Dr. Samuel Johnson,* in *The Early Biographies of Samuel Johnson,* ed. O. M. Brack, Jr., and R. E. Kelley, (Iowa City: University of Iowa Press, 1974), p. 18. (Hereafter cited as *The Early Biographies.*)

5. Each of the following studies has made a substantial contribution to this subject though none is devoted exclusively to it: J. W. Krutch, *Samuel Johnson* (New York: Henry Holt, 1944), esp. pp. 163–65, 250–52, 545–50; B. H. Bronson, *Johnson Agonistes and Other Essays* (Cambridge: Harvard University Press, 1946), esp. the titular essay; James Clifford, *Young Sam Johnson* (New York: McGraw-Hill, 1955), indispensable for Johnson's youthful religious attitudes; Robert Voitle, *Samuel Johnson the Moralist* (Cambridge: Harvard University Press, 1961); Arieh Sachs, *Passionate Intelligence* (Baltimore: Johns Hopkins University Press, 1967), esp. pp. 109–19; Donald Greene, *Samuel Johnson* (New York: Twayne Publishers, 1970), esp. pp. 121–47; James Gray, *Johnson's Sermons* (Oxford: Oxford University Press, 1972), esp. pp. 131–82; Richard Schwartz, *Samuel Johnson and the Problem of Evil* (Madison:

University of Wisconsin Press, 1975); and W. Jackson Bate, *Samuel Johnson* (New York: Harcourt Brace Jovanovich, 1977), esp. pp. 450–61.

6. Maurice Quinlan, *Samuel Johnson: A Layman's Religion* (Madison: University of Wisconsin Press, 1964).

7. Chester Chapin, *The Religious Thought of Samuel Johnson* (Ann Arbor: University of Michigan Press, 1968).

8. Bronson, *Johnson Agonistes*, p. 41.

Chapter 1

1. *Letters*, no. 578.

2. *Life*, 4:429.

3. Samuel Johnson, *Sermons*, ed. by Jean H. Hagstrum and James Gray, in *The Yale Edition of the Works of Samuel Johnson* (New Haven: Yale University Press, 1958–), 14:161.

4. Samuel Johnson, *Rasselas*, in *The Works of Samuel Johnson, L.L.D.* (Oxford, 1825), ed. Arthur Murphy, 3:337.

5. See Life, 4:394–99; see also H. L. Thrale, *Anecdotes*, in *Johnsonian Miscellanies*, ed. G. B. Hill, 2 vols., (1897; reprinted, New York: Barnes and Noble, 1966), 1:296–97. (Hereafter cited as *JM*.)

6. Krutch, *Samuel Johnson*, p. 1; Bate, *Samuel Johnson*, pp. 480–99; Schwartz, *Samuel Johnson*, pp. 43–50.

7. Samuel Johnson, *Diaries, Prayers, Annals*, ed. by E. L. McAdam, Jr. with Donald and Mary Hyde, in *The Yale Edition of the Works of Samuel Johnson* (New Haven: Yale University Press, 1958–), 1:3–6. (Hereafter cited as *Works*.)

8. Clifford, *Sam Johnson*, p. 9.

9. *Works*, 4:11.

10. Clifford, *Sam Johnson*, p. 20; *Life*, 1:35–40.

11. George Irwin, *Samuel Johnson: A Personality in Conflict* (Auckland: Auckland University Press, 1971), pp. 90–91.

12. *Works*, 1:7-8.

13. Samuel Johnson, *The Rambler*, ed. by W. J. Bate and Albrecht B. Strauss in *The Yale Edition of the Works of Samuel Johnson* (New Haven: Yale University Press, 1958–), 4:143–48.

14. Schwartz, *Samuel Johnson*, pp. 61–65, 72.

15. *Works*, 3:133.

16. See *Rambler* 108, 155, 180; *Idler* 27; *Adventurer* 111.

17. John Wain, *Samuel Johnson* (New York: Viking Press, 1974), pp. 43–44.

18. *Life,* 1:73–74.

19. *Life,* 1:77.

20. *Works,* 1:27.

21. *Life,* 1:63–4.

22. *Life,* 1:35; Katharine C. Balderston, "Dr. Johnson and William Law," *PMLA* 75 (September 1960):382–94.

23. *Life,* 1:64.

24. *Life,* 4:215.

25. Chapin, *Religious Thought,* p. 40.

26. *Life,* 1:67–69.

27. *Works,* 1:10.

28. Clifford, *Sam Johnson,* p. 23.

29. *Life,* 4:215.

30. *Life,* 1:67.

31. *JM,* 1:157–58.

32. *Life,* 1:444.

33. *Life,* 1:67–68.

34. Clifford, *Sam Johnson,* p. 92,

35. Sir John Hawkins, *The Life of Samuel Johnson* (London, 1787), p. 18.

36. *Life,* 1:68.

37. William Law, *A Serious Call to a Devout and Holy Life* (1729; reprint ed., London: Everyman, 1951), p. 162.

38. Ibid., p. 7.

39. Ibid., p. 121.

40. Ibid., p. 117.

41. *Life,* 1:68–69, 2:122.

42. Quinlan, *Samuel Johnson,* p. 26.

43. Chapin, *Religious Thought,* pp. 40–41.

44. Ortega Y. Gasset, *The Revolt of the Masses* (New York: Norton, 1932), p. 157.

45. *Works,* 1:269.

46. Ernest Becker, *The Denial of Death* (New York: Free Press, 1973), p. 90. I would like to record here a general debt to Ernest Becker's provocative study, which helped me to see Johnson's religious life in new ways.

47. William James, *The Varieties of Religious Experience* (1902; reprint ed., New York: Collier-Macmillan, 1961), p. 165.

Chapter 2

1. *Life,* 2:27.
2. Chapin, *Religious Thought,* pp. 155–56.
3. *Life,* 3:316–17.
4. *Life,* 1:398.
5. Stuart Gerry Brown, "Dr. Johnson and the Religious Problem," *English Studies* 20 (February/April 1938): 1–17.
6. *Life,* 3:317.
7. Samuel Johnson, *Sermons,* ed. by Jean H. Hagstrum and James Gray in *The Yale Edition of the Works of Samuel Johnson* (New Haven: Yale University Press, 1958–), 3:29. All citations from Johnson's *Sermons* derive from this text. To reduce the number of notes I have included the number of the sermon in the text.
8. *Life,* 3:200.
9. *Life,* 5:180.
10. *Life,* 4:299.
11. *Life,* 2:82.
12. *Life,* 2:104.
13. I wish to express a general debt to Chester Chapin, *Religious Thought,* for information on this aspect of this important subject; see esp. pp. 112–17.
14. Ibid., p. 115.
15. *Life,* 2:104.
16. *Life,* 3:290–91.
17. Chapin, *Religious Thought,* pp. 115–16.
18. Schwartz, *Samuel Johnson,* p. 38.
19. Samuel Johnson, *Idler and Adventurer,* ed. by W. J. Bate, J. M. Bullitt, and L. F. Powell, in *The Yale Edition of the Works of Samuel Johnson* (New Haven: Yale University Press, 1958–) 2:275. Hereafter cited as *Idler and Adventurer.*
20. *Life,* 5:117.
21. *Life,* 5:211.
22. *JM,* 1:268.
23. *Life,* 3:317.
24. *Life,* 3:188; 3:363.
25. Schwartz, *Samuel Johnson,* p. 43.
26. *Idler and Adventurer,* 2:451–2.
27. Ernest C. Mossner, *The Life of David Hume* (Austin: University of Texas Press, 1954), pp. 393, 438, 586. Mossner makes clear that Johnson had been in Hume's presence twice, once in

1762 when Johnson snubbed Hume and once in 1763 when they had both been dinner guests of the royal chaplain's at Saint James. Mossner (p. 586, n. 3) also speculates that Johnson might have been a guest of Hume, either during the period 1766–68 or perhaps in 1776. Johnson himself made few explicit references to Hume's writing in his own work, though his remarks in conversation reveal that he had read enough of—or about—Hume on religious matters so that he could attack him with confidence. Johnson refers only once to the *Treatise of Human Nature* (*Life*, 1:127) and twice to the *Political Discourses* (*Life*, 2:53; 5:31), and admits that as of 1773 he had not read Hume's *History of England* (*Life*, 2:236).

28. *Life*, 1:444–45.

29. Donald T. Siebert, "Johnson and Hume on Miracles," *Journal of History of Ideas* 36 (1975):543–47.

30. Charles E. Noyes, "Samuel Johnson: Student of Hume," *University of Mississippi Studies in English* 3 (1962):91–94.

31. *Life*, 1:428; see also Noyes, "Samuel Johnson," on this subject.

32. *Life*, 1:398.

33. David Hume, "Of Miracles," in *An Enquiry Concerning Human Understanding*, ed. L. A. Selby-Bigge. (1777; reprint ed., Oxford: Oxford University Press, 1966), p. 127. (Hereafter cited as *Enquiry*.)

34. David Hume, "Of a Particular Providence and of a Future State," in *Enquiry*, as cited above, pp. 136–146.

35. *Life*, 5:274.

36. Chapin, *Religious Thought*, p. 88.

37. Ibid.

38. *Inquiry*, p. 140.

39. See Ernest C. Mossner, *The Forgotten Hume* (New York: Columbia University Press, 1943), esp. pp. 181–209, and *Life of David Hume*, chaps. 39 and 40. See also Norman Kemp Smith's introduction, appendixes, and supplement to his edition of Hume's *Dialogues* (New York: Social Science Publishers, 1948). Of the many articles on this elusive subject the following are helpful: James Noxon, "Hume's Agnosticism," *Philosophical Review* 73, no. 3 (1964): 248–61 and Keith E. Yandell, "Hume on Religious Belief," in *Hume: A Re-Evaluation*, ed. Donald W. Livingston and James T. King, (New York: Fordham University Press, 1976), pp. 109–25.

40. *Life*, 3:154.

41. *Life*, 4:299.

42. *JM*, 1:277.
43. *Works*, 1:123.
44. *Life*, 2:124.
45. Quinlan, *Samuel Johnson*, p. x.
46. *Works*, 1:64.
47. See also *Rambler* 7, 71, 110, 203.
48. *JM*, 1:223–24.
49. *Life*, 3:294–95.
50. *Letters*, no. 938.
51. *Life*, 1:64–65.
52. *Works*, 1:119.
53. *JM*, 1:148.
54. *Life*, 1:35.
55. *Life*, 2:440; *Life*, 3:26.
56. *Life*, 1:463.
57. *Works*, 1:257.
58. W. B. C. Watkins, *In Perilous Balance* (Princeton: Princeton University Press, 1939), p. 65.
59. Bate, *Samuel Johnson*, pp. 263–64.
60. *Works*, 1:46.
61. *Works*, 1:80.
62. *Works*, 1:138.
63. James, *Religious Experience*, pp. 78–142. The following discussion derives almost entirely from James's treatment of this subject.

Chapter 3

1. *JM*, 1:209.
2. Hawkins, *Samuel Johnson*, pp. 162–63; Boswell's *Life*, 5:17. See also the short biographical pieces collected in *The Early Biographies* cited earlier, almost all of which attest to Johnson's piety.
3. *Works*, 1:266.
4. *Life*, 4:395–99.
5. *Life*, 1:67.
6. *Works*, 1:306–7.
7. *Works*, 1:407–11. It should also be noted how much of this religious reading he made use of when he came to provide examples of usage in the *Dictionary*.
8. Law, *A Serious Call*, pp. 18–19.

9. Ibid., p. 178.
10. Ibid., pp. 116–17.
11. Ibid., p. 7.
12. *Life*, 3:401.
13. *Life*, 1:67.
14. *Works*, 1:267; 1:309.
15. *Life*, 2:458.
16. *Life*, 2:458, n. 3.
17. *Works*, 1:62.
18. Johnson here recommends William Lowth and Simon Patrick for their respective studies of the Old Testament and Henry Hammond for his *Paraphrase and Annotations in the New Testament*. See *Life*, 3:58.
19. *Works*, 1:151.
20. *Works*, 1:268; *JM*, 2:384.
21. *Life*, 3:298.
22. *Works*, 1:103.
23. *Works*, 1:83.
24. *Works*, 1:413. See the long note by the editors on this subject.
25. *Works*, 1:409.
26. Hawkins, *Samuel Johnson*, pp. 541–43.
27. *Works*, 1:97; *Life*, 2:178.
28. *Life*, 5:68.
29. *Works*, 1:131.
30. *JM*, 2:86, n. 3.
31. *Life*, 4:293.
32. *Works*, 1:37–8.
33. *Works*, 1:54.
34. *Works*, 1:56.
35. *Works*, 1:122–23.
36. See also Sermon 10 in *Works*, 14.
37. *Life*, 2:435.
38. *Life*, 4:376–77.
39. *Life*, 4:295.

Chapter 4

1. *Life*, 4:429.
2. *Life*, 3:298–99.

3. *Life,* 2:106.
4. *Life,* 3:153; *Life,* 2:93.
5. *Life,* 3:154.
6. *Life,* 3:153.
7. *Life,* 5:397.
8. *Letters,* no. 943.
9. J. H. Hagstrum, "On Dr. Johnson's Fear of Death," *English Literary History* 14 (December 1947): 308–19.
10. *Life,* 2:298.
11. *Life,* 4:278.
12. *Life,* 3:154.
13. *Life,* 3:295.
14. Henry David Thoreau, *Walden* (1854; reprint ed., Boston: Houghton-Mifflin, 1906), pp. 100–101.
15. *Life,* 4:394.
16. *Life,* 2:440.
17. W. Jackson Bate, *The Achievement of Samuel Johnson* (New York: Oxford University Press, 1955), pp. 93–94.
18. Soren Kierkegaard, *Fear and Trembling* and *The Sickness Unto Death,* trans. Walter Lowrie (1843, 1849; reprint ed., 2 vols in 1 New York: Doubleday Anchor, 1954), p. 155.
19. *Life,* 3:415.
20. *Life,* 5:307–8.
21. Hawkins, *Samuel Johnson,* p. 404.
22. *JM,* 1:292.
23. *JM,* 2:429.
24. *JM,* 1:204.
25. *JM,* 1:219.
26. *JM,* 2:416.
27. Hawkins, *Samuel Johnson,* p. 404.
28. *Life,* 2:66.
29. *Life,* 1:300.
30. *Life,* 4:145.
31. *Letters,* no. 541.
32. *Life,* 4:147.
33. *Life,* 1:204.
34. *Life,* 2:361.
35. *Life,* 2:359.
36. *Life,* 3:57.
37. *Life,* 4:50.
38. *Life,* 1:490.

39. *Life*, 1:103–4, n. 3.
40. *Life*, 3:42.
41. *Life*, 3:327.
42. *JM*, 2:333.
43. *Life*, 1:66.
44. Samuel Johnson, *Rasselas*, in *The Works of Samuel Johnson, L.L.D.*, ed. Arthur Murphy, 11 vols. (Oxford, 1825), 3:422–23.
45. *Life*, 1:65.
46. *Life*, 1:65; *Life*, 5:215.
47. Law, *A Serious Call*, p. 51.
48. Becker, *Denial of Death*, p. 259.
49. Paul Fussell, *Samuel Johnson and the Life of Writing* (New York: Harcourt Brace, 1971), pp. 91–97.
50. Bate, *Samuel Johnson*, pp. 231–39; 371–89.
51. *Life*, 4:427.
52. *Life*, 1:64.
53. Geoffrey Tillotson, "Time in Rasselas," in *Bicentenary Essays on Rasselas*, ed. M. Wahba, (Cairo, 1959), pp. 97–103.
54. Works, 1:38, 41, 63, 99, 228.
55. Fussell, *Samuel Johnson*, p. 112.
56. *Works*, 1:50.

Chapter 5

1. Samuel Johnson, *The Vanity of Human Wishes*, in *Works*, 6:90–109.
2. Bate, *Samuel Johnson*, p. 280.
3. Hawkins, *Samuel Johnson*, p. 202.
4. Mary Lascelles, "Johnson and Juvenal," in *New Light on Dr. Johnson*, ed. F. W. Hilles, (Hamden: Archon Books, 1967), pp. 35–57.
5. F. W. Hilles, "Johnson's Poetic Fire," in *From Sensibility to Romanticism* (Oxford: Oxford University Press, 1965), p. 75.
6. Samuel Johnson, *Poems*, ed. E. L. McAdam, Jr. with George Milne, in *The Yale Edition of the Works of Samuel Johnson* (New Haven: Yale University Press, 1958-   ), p. xviii.
7. Leopold Damrosch, *Samuel Johnson and the Tragic Sense* (Princeton: Princeton University Press, 1972), p. 154.
8. Samuel Johnson, *A Review of Soames Jenyns's A Free Inquiry into the Nature and Origin of Evil*, in *The Works of Samuel Johnson*, ed. Arthur Murphy, 12 vols., (London, 1806), 8:48.

9. Quoted in *Poems,* p. 46.

10. Ian Jack, *Augustan Satire* (Oxford: Oxford University Press, 1952), p. 136.

11. *Lives,* 1:202–4.

12. Alfred North Whitehead, *Religion in the Making* (New York: Macmillan, 1926), p. 31.

13. *Life,* 1:342.

14. Gwin Kolb, "The Structure of *Rasselas,*" *PMLA* 66 (September 1951): 698–717.

15. Alvin Whitley, "The Comedy of *Rasselas,*" *English Literary History* 23 (March 1956): 48–70.

16. Earl Wasserman, "Johnson's *Rasselas:* Implicit Contexts," *Journal of English and Germanic Philology* 74 (1975): 1–25.

17. Emrys Jones, "The Artistic Form of *Rasselas,*" *Review of English Studies* n.s. 18 (November 1967): 387–401.

18. Patrick O'Flaherty, "Dr. Johnson as Equivocator: The Meaning of *Rasselas,*" *Modern Language Quarterly* 31 (1970):195–208.

Chapter 6

1. *Life,* 1:353–58.
2. *Works,* 1:73.
3. *Works,* 1:76–7.
4. *Life,* 1:483.
5. *Works,* 1:81.
6. *Works,* 1:105–8.
7. *JM,* 1:234.
8. Bate, *Samuel Johnson,* pp. 384–88.
9. Ibid., p. 383.
10. *Works,* 1:91–92.
11. *Works,* 1:114.
12. *Works,* 1:363.
13. *Works,* 1:69. See editorial notes on this subject.
14. *Works,* 1:107.
15. *Life,* 4:226; Gray, *Sermons,* pp. 92–114.
16. Richard Baxter, *The Autobiography of Richard Baxter,* ed. J. M. Lloyd Thomas, (1696; reprint ed., abr., London: J. M. Dent, 1925), p. 107. All of the following quotations derive from this text. See especially pp. 103–32.
17. Chapin, *Religious Thought,* pp. 118–40.

18. *Works,* 1:115.
19. *Works,* 1:122–23.
20. *Works,* 1:269.

Chapter 7

1. Hawkins, *Samuel Johnson,* p. 592.
2. *Life,* 2:106–7.
3. *Life,* 4:256.
4. *Life,* 4:369.
5. *Letters,* no. 655.
6. *Letters,* no. 932.
7. *Letters,* no. 995.
8. *Letters,* no. 943.
9. *Life,* 4:299.
10. *Letters,* no. 938.
11. *Works,* 1:383.
12. *Life,* 4:298-99.
13. *Works,* 1:414.
14. *Letters,* no. 929.1.
15. Hawkins, *Samuel Johnson,* pp. 564-65.
16. *Ibid., pp. 565–66.*
17. *Letters,* no. 935.
18. *Life,* 4:272.
19. *Life,* 4:278.
20. Hawkins, *Samuel Johnson,* p. 583.
21. Chester Chapin, "Samuel Johnson's 'Wonderful Experience,'" in *Johnsonian Studies,* ed. Magdi Wahba, (Cairo, 1962), p. 58. Chapin remarks here that Johnson could not help but regard his remarkable recovery "as a sign that this hope had not been altogether vain—that his repentance had been of such depth and sincerity as to have found favor in the sight of God."
22. *Letters,* no. 875.
23. *Works,* 1:393.
24. *Life,* 4:293–94.
25. *Life,* 5:88.
26. Quinlan, *Samuel Johnson,* pp. 47–49.
27. *Life,* 4:124–25. This entire argument Johnson dictated to Boswell at the latter's request.
28. Quinlan, *Samuel Johnson,* pp. 57–59.

29. *Works,* 1:309.

30. *Works,* 1:305.

31. *Letters,* no. 1003.1

32. *Letters,* no. 1021.

33. *JM,* 2:382–87.

34. *JM,* 2:146.

35. Hawkins, *Samuel Johnson,* p. 580.

36. *Life, 4:394.*

37. *Hawkins, Samuel Johnson,* p. 588.

38. *JM,* 2:156.

39. *Works,* 1:417–18.

40. Maurice Quinlan, "The Rumor of Dr. Johnson's Conversion," *Review of Religion* 12 (March 1948): 243–261.

41. Donald Greene, "Dr. Johnson's 'Late Conversion': A Reconsideration," in *Johnsonian Studies,* ed. Magdi Wahba, pp. 61–92.

42. Hawkins, *Samuel Johnson,* p. 581.

Bibliography

Bate, W. Jackson. *The Achievement of Samuel Johnson.* New York: Oxford University Press, 1955.

———. *Samuel Johnson.* New York: Harcourt Brace Jovanovich, 1977.

Becker, Ernest. *The Denial of Death.* New York: Free Press, 1973.

Boswell, James. *The Life of Samuel Johnson, LLD.* Edited by G. B. Hill and revised by L. F. Powell. 6 vols. Oxford: Oxford University Press, 1934–50.

Bronson, Bertrand. *Johnson Agonistes and Other Essays.* Cambridge: Harvard University Press, 1946.

Chapin, Chester. *The Religious Thought of Samuel Johnson.* Ann Arbor: University of Michigan Press, 1968.

Clifford, James. *Young Sam Johnson.* New York: McGraw-Hill, 1955.

———. *Dictionary Johnson.* New York: McGraw-Hill, 1979.

Damrosch, Leopold. *Samuel Johnson and the Tragic Sense.* Princeton: Princeton University Press, 1972.

Fussell, Paul. *Samuel Johnson and the Life of Writing.* New York: Harcourt Brace Jovanovich, 1971.

Gray, James. *Johnson's Sermons.* Oxford: Clarendon Press, 1972.

Greene, Donald. *Samuel Johnson.* New York: Twayne Publishers, 1970.

Hawkins, Sir John. *The Life of Samuel Johnson.* London, 1787.

Irwin, George. *Samuel Johnson: A Personality in Conflict.* Auckland: Auckland University Press, 1971.

James, William. *The Varieties of Religious Experience.* New York, 1902; rpt. New York: Collier-Macmillan, 1961.

Johnson, Samuel. *The Works of Samuel Johnson, LLD.* 11 vols. Oxford, 1825.

———. *The Yale Edition of the Works of Samuel Johnson.* 11 vols. New Haven: Yale University Press, 1958—.

———. *The Lives of the Poets.* Edited by G. B. Hill, 3 vols. Oxford, 1905.

———. *The Letters of Samuel Johnson.* Edited by R. W. Chapman. 3 vols. Oxford, 1952.

Johnsonian Miscellanies. Edited by G. B. Hill. 2 vols. Oxford: The Clarendon Press, 1897; rpt. New York: Barnes and Noble, 1966.

Johnsonian Studies. Edited by Magdi Wahba. Cairo, 1962.

The Early Biographies of Samuel Johnson. Edited by O. M. Brack, Jr. and R. E. Kelley. Iowa City: University of Iowa Press, 1974.

Krutch, Joseph W. *Samuel Johnson.* New York: Henry Holt, 1944.

Law, William. *A Serious Call to a Devout and Holy Life.* London, 1729; rpt. London: Everyman, 1951.

Mossner, Ernest. *The Life of David Hume.* Austin: University of Texas Press, 1954.

———. *The Forgotten Hume.* New York: Columbia University Press, 1943.

Piozzi, Hester L. *Anecdotes of the Late Samuel Johnson, LLD.* Edited by G. B. Hill. In *Johnsonian Miscellanies,* vol. 1. Oxford, 1897.

Quinlan, Maurice. *Samuel Johnson: A Layman's Religion.* Madison: University of Wisconsin Press, 1964.

Sachs, Arieh. *Passionate Intelligence.* Baltimore: Johns Hopkins Press, 1967.

Schwartz, Richard. *Samuel Johnson and the Problem of Evil.* Madison: University of Wisconsin Press, 1975.

Voitle, Robert. *Samuel Johnson the Moralist.* Cambridge: Harvard University Press, 1961.

Wain, John. *Samuel Johnson.* New York: Viking Press, 1974.

Watkins, W. B. *In Perilous Balance.* Oxford: Oxford University Press, 1939.

Whitehead, A. N. *Religion in the Making.* New York: Macmillan, 1926.

Index

Absurdist view of life, 126-29
Activity, Value of, 90-92
Adams, William, 38, 51, 54, 131, 155, 156
  on SJ's last illness, 148, 150
  on SJ's melancholy, 133
Anglican Church (Church of England), 10, 15, 25, 32, 38, 42, 76
  Articles of Religion, 41
  rationalism in, 53n
Annihilation, definition of, 37-38
Anxiety, 89-90

Balderston, Katharine, 23
Barber, Francis, 152, 154, 160
Bate, W. Jackson, 59, 89, 106, 112, 135, 136
Baxter, Richard, 76, 140, 141-44
Beattie, James, *Essay on Truth*, 50
Becker, Ernest, 32-33, 104
Beckett, Samuel, 131
Bible, SJ's reading of, 66, 73-74, 158-59
Bible, New Testament, 74, 158, 161
  Corinthians I, 113
  Luke, 105
Birmingham, 23, 92
Blacklock, Thomas, 52n
Book of Common Prayer, 65, 73, 74-75, 78
  SJ plans book on use of, 75
Boothby, Hill, 53n
Boswell, James, 23, 31, 71, 72, 95, 136, 154
  and Hume's argument against miracles, 47
  SJ advises him on Scottish law, 94
  on SJ as gladiator, 86, 100, 147
  SJ's character summarized, 9-10, 106-107
  on SJ's conversation, 96
  on SJ's depression (hypochondria), 22-23
  on SJ's piety, 65
  on SJ's preparation for death, 147, 153, 155-56, 161, 163
  on SJ's second breakdown, 133
  on SJ's view of madness and melancholy, 99-100
Bowles, William, 52n
Bramhall, John, 40-41
Brocklesby, Dr. Richard, 161
Bronson, Bertrand, 11
Brown, S. G., 35
Browne, Sir Thomas, 53, 103
Bunyan, John, 61, 84
  Pilgrim's Progress, 111
Burton, Robert, 53, 58
  Anatomy of Melancholy, 91
Butler, Joseph, 52n, 53

Cave, William, *Apostolici, or Lives of the Primitive Fathers*, 75-76
Chambers, Robert, 94

Chapin, Chester, 10, 23-24, 31, 41-42, 50, 52, 53n, 142
Cheyne, George, 58
Christ, SJ's attitude toward, 156-59
Christmas, observance of, 71, 72
Church attendance, 25-26, 69-70
Church Fathers, 73, 75-76, 77
Clarke, Samuel, 10, 35, 40, 41, 48, 52n, 53, 77, 158, 161
  A Demonstration of the Being and Attributes of God, 35
Clifford, James, 18, 19, 28
Club, the, 36
Communion, 69, 70-71
  before SJ's death, 156, 159, 160-61, 163
Conrad, Joseph, *Heart of Darkness,* 31
Cowper, William, 62

Damnation, 24, 54
Damrosch, Leopold, 114
Death: SJ's attitude toward, 18, 121
  SJ's fear of, 18, 86-90, 147-48, 151
  SJ's preparation for, 146-64
Defoe, Daniel, 65
Deism, 51, 52n, 53
Depravity, natural, 43
Desmoulins, Mrs., 154
Determinism, 40
Devotion, 63-64, 66
  definitions of, 63-64
  in Law's *Serious Call,* 67-68
  SJ's practices of, 68-83
Dodd, Dr., 86-87
Dublin, Trinity College, honorary degree for SJ, 136

Easter, observance of, 71, 72, 131-32, 134, 137-38, 156, 159
Eliot, T. S., 53
Evangelical movement, 53n
Evil, 42-46, 115
  moral and physical, 42-44

Faith, 35-44, 51, 85, 90, 117
  crisis of, 139-45
Ford, Cornelius, 21
Free will, 39-42, 88

Freud, Sigmund, 89
Fussell, Paul, 108

Gaubius, Professor, 100
George III, King, 136
God: in Deism, 52n
  dependence on, 112-15, 122-23
  evil not created by, 42-43
  fear of, 115
  goodness of, 38
  justice and mercy of, 36-38, 50
  of Nature and of New Testament, 44
  of once-born and twice-born souls, 60-61
  SJ's belief in, 35-44
Goldsmith, Oliver, 94
Gray, James, 52n, 141
Greene, Donald, 163
Grotius, Hugo, 48, 51
  De Veritate Religionis Christi, 35, 66, 73

Hagstrum, Jean, 87
Hammond, Henry, 80-81, 163
Happiness: in *Rasselas,* 124-29
  search for, 124-25
  uncertainty of, 123
Hawkins, Sir John, 28-29, 76, 78, 93, 113, 146
  on SJ's last days, 152-53, 160, 161, 162, 164
Heberden, Dr. William, 153
Hector, Edmund, 95
Hilles, F. W., 114
Hobbes, Thomas, 40, 42
Holy days, observance of, 69, 71-72
Hooker, Richard, 10, 53, 76, 143
  Laws of Ecclesiastical Polity, 101
Hume, David: death of, 87
  on miracles, SJ's response to, 46-52
  SJ's attitude toward, 27, 47
  An Enquiry Concerning Human Understanding, 47, 49

Imagination: as enemy of reason, 102
  SJ's interpretation of, 59-60, 102

Immortality, 44, 46
hope for, 123-24
Indolence, 80
Irwin, George, 19

Jack, Ian, 116
Jackson, Harry, 95
James, William, 33, 53, 117
on once-born and twice-born souls, 60-61
Jenyns, Soame, 42, 115
Job and physical evil, 42
Johnson, Elizabeth (Tetty), wife of SJ, 79
death, 59, 72
SJ's prayer after her death, 59
Johnson, Michael, father of SJ, 18-20, 22, 23
married life, 19-20
SJ's melancholy inherited from, 58, 100
Johnson, Samuel:
activity, mental and physical, 90-92
attitude toward his parents, 18-20
belief in God, 35-44
charity, 93-94
church attendance, 25-26, 69-70
compassion for others, 92-93
conversation, 96-97
conversion, rumor of, 162-63
devotional practices, 68-83
diseases and infirmities, 17-18
diversions, need of, 95-99
doubts and fears in religion, 10-11, 16-17, 31, 32, 34, 54-57, 84-86
drinking habits, 98-99
early life, 17-18
excellence, desire for, 19
failure to achieve religious goals, 136-41
failure to attend church services, 69-70
faith, 35-44, 85, 90, 111
faith, crisis of, 139-45
faith, need for, 117
faith rediscovered, 32-34
fear of death, 18, 86-90, 147-48, 151
fear of loneliness (solitude), 94, 97
fear of madness, 99-101, 103-104, 135, 138-39
fear of misspent life, 104-109, 138-39
friendships, 94-95, 154
as gladiator against fears, 86, 100, 147
guilt feelings, 19, 58-59, 63, 69-70
honorary degrees, 136
last illness, 151-53, 160-62
last prayer, 162
meditation, private, 68, 69, 80
melancholy (acute depression), 16, 19, 22-23, 57-62, 105, 106
melancholy, second breakdown, 131-45
observance of holy days, 69, 71-72
pension, 136
pessimism, 16-17, 19, 61-62
poverty as disadvantage, 21-22
prayer, habits of, 55, 59, 60, 68, 70, 73, 75, 77-80
prayers at beginning of writings, 108-109
prayers in last year of life, 149-50, 155, 160, 161, 162
preparation for death, 146-64
as a psychologist, 102-103
quasi-mystical experience before death, 151-54, 164
reasoning from particular to general, 103
record of spiritual progress, 79-80
religion developed in youth, 25-28
religion learned from his mother, 24-25, 28, 65-66
religion rediscovered in sickness, 23-24, 31-33
salvation, hope for, 146, 148, 153-55, 159
scruples, religious, 139-40

search for meaning of life, 111-30
skepticism, notes on, 150-51
study of mind, 101-104
study of religious books, 72-77
as talker against religion, 27-28
travels, 92
will, 160, 164
zest for life, 88-90
Writings
Adventurer, The, 45, 121-22, 136
diary, private, 17, 18, 32, 69, 134, 144-45
Dictionary, 33, 37, 39, 40, 63, 76, 79, 80, 90n, 91, 100, 101, 105, 106, 109, 115, 136, 139, 163
Idler, The, 43, 87, 91, 97, 104, 129, 136
journals, private, 19-20, 131-32, 134
Life of Waller, 116
Lives of the Poets, 63, 106
London, 115-16
Prayers and Meditations, 64-65, 73, 78-80, 83, 107-108
Rambler, The, 20, 64, 89, 90-91, 101-102, 103, 105, 108, 109, 118-24, 136, 159
Rasselas, 11, 16, 99, 100, 102, 107, 112, 124-30, 136
Sermons, 35-38, 43-46, 55, 70, 71, 81, 82, 90, 106, 108
Shakespeare, edition of, 104, 131, 136
Vanity of Human Wishes, The, 11, 112-16, 129, 130, 133, 136
Johnson, Sarah, mother of SJ, 18-19, 87, 88
death, 129
married life, 19-20
religious training of SJ, 24-25, 28, 65-66
Jones, Emrys, 128
Juvenal, 113-18

Kierkegaard, Soren, 32-33, 53, 89-90
Knowledge: perfect, futility in pursuit of, 102
virtue promoted by, 101
Knowles, Mary (Mrs. Thomas), 57, 74 and Quakerism, 84-85
Kolb, Gwin, 124-25
Krutch, Joseph Wood, 88

Langton, Bennet, 94
Lascelles, Mary, 113
Law, William, 10, 64, 73, 77, 130, 157
A Serious Call to a Devout and Holy Life, 23, 29-33, 66-68, 84, 104, 136-37
Levet, Robert, 97, 154
Lichfield, 17, 22, 25, 92, 94
grammar school, 21, 27
SJ's church attendance in boyhood, 69-70
Lindsay, John, 53n
Locke, John, 39
Lyttelton, Lord, death of, predicted, 150

MacLeod, Lady, 43
Madness: melancholy related to, 99-100;
SJ's concern for the insane, 94
SJ's fear of, 99-101, 103-104
Meditation, SJ's practice of, 68, 69, 80
Melancholy, 16, 19, 22-23, 57-62, 105, 106
madness related to, 99-100
Methodists, 53n
Milton, John, 101
Paradise Lost, 40, 43
Mind: moral discipline of, 119-20
SJ's study of, 101-104, 123
Miracles, Hume's argument on, and
SJ's response, 46-53
Misery: and evil, 42-46
radical, 23

Necessity (free will), 39
Nelson, Robert, *Companion for the Festivals and Fasts of the Church of England,* 72
Newman, John Henry, 61

Noyes, Charles E., 48

O'Flaherty, Patrick, 128, 130
Ogden, Samuel, 73
Once-born and twice-born souls, 60-61
Ortega y Gasset, Jose, 15, 17, 31
Oxford, 92
  honorary degree for SJ, 136
  Pembroke College, SJ's gift to, 160
  SJ at, 20-22, 28, 33
  SJ leaves, 17, 21-22

Paradise, Peter, 107
Pascal, Blaise, 34
Pearson, John, 48
  An Exposition of the Creed, 35
Pessimism, 16-17, 19, 61-62
Piety, 63-83
Politian, Angelus, 91
Pope, Alexander, 17, 19, 123
  Essay on Man, 115
Porter, Lucy, 153
Prayer: in Law's *Serious Call*, 67-68
  SJ considers making anthology of, 155-56
  SJ's habits of, 55, 68, 70, 73, 75, 77-80
Predestination, 88
Protestantism, 10
Psychology, SJ's understanding of, 102-103
Puritans, 76, 77

Quakers, 71, 84-85
Quinlan, Maurice, 10, 31, 55, 157, 158, 162-63

Rationalism, 53, 54
  and Deism, 51, 52n
Rationalization and virtue, 101-102, 119
Reason: definition of, 101
  imagination as enemy of, 102
  power of, 119-20
Repentance, 55-56, 80-82, 163
Retirement from the world, 81
Reynolds, Sir Joshua, 92, 96, 98, 148
Ryland, John, 159, 160, 161-62

Salvation, 44, 54-57
  SJ's hope for, 146, 148, 153-55, 159
Satan and moral evil, 42
Savage, Richard, 94
Schwartz, Richard, 43, 45
Scott, Sir Walter, 113
Siebert, Donald, 47-48
Scruples, 139-40
Self-knowledge and self-control, 123
Seward, Anna, 23
Shakespeare, William: *Macbeth*, 161-62
  works edited by SJ, 104, 131, 136
Sidney, Sir Philip, 119
South, Robert, 39
  Sermons on Prayer, 40
Spottiswoode, John, 98
Sterne, Laurence, 126
Stoicism, 113-16, 118
Strahan, George, 64-65, 140, 160, 162, 163
Swift, Jonathan, 43, 65, 123
Swinfen, Dr., 18, 23, 58

Taylor, Jeremy, 139
Taylor, John, 95, 155
Thomas a Kempis, 73
Thoreau, Henry David, 89
Thrale, Henry, 95, 154
Thrale, Hester Lynch (later Mrs. Piozzi), 58, 87, 93, 95, 100, 154
  SJ's break with, 154
  and SJ's death, 148, 149
  on SJ's early religion, 26-27
  on SJ's fears and doubts, 54, 56, 57
  on SJ's nervous breakdown, 134-35
  and SJ's padlock, 135
  on SJ's piety, 64
  on SJ's view of depravity, 43

Thrale, Queeney, letters from SJ, 9, 151-52
Thrale family, 92, 95, 131, 134, 136
Tillotson, Geoffrey, 107
Tillotson, John, 90n
Time, use of, 104-109
Tolstoi, Leo, 61

Unhappiness (misery), 42-46
  self-created, 45
Ussher, James, 76

Virtue: knowledge related to, 101
  pursuit of, 119-22

Wain, John, 21
Wasserman, Earl, 127
Watkins, W. B. C., 59
Wesley, John, 53n
Whitehead, Alfred North, 84, 117
Whitley, Alvin, 125
Whole Duty of Man, The (Anonymous), 25, 65-66, 73
Willey, Basil, 52n
Williams, Anna, 97, 98-99, 154
Windham, William, 74, 161